Hearing God

8 Steps to Understanding the Bible

KNOFEL STATON

STANDARD PUBLISHING
Cincinnati, Ohio

Cover design by SchultzWard, Inc.

The Standard Publishing Company, Cincinnati, Ohio.
A division of Standex International Corporation.

©1993 by The Standard Publishing Company.
All rights reserved.
Printed in the United States of America.

00 99 98 97 96 95 94 93   5 4 3 2 1

Library of Congress Cataloging in Publication data:

Staton, Knofel.
    Hearing God : 8 steps to understanding the Bible / Knofel
        Staton.
        p. cm.
    ISBN 0-7847-0052-4
    1. Bible--Study and teaching.   I. Title.
BS600.2.S74   1993
220'.07—dc20   93-1342
                                                      CIP

Contents

In Appreciation

Some people write anonymously, but no one can write a book autonomously. And I certainly have not and do not. God has used many people who have modeled effective Bible study for me.

Dr. Marion Henderson, professor at Lincoln Christian College, demonstrated in his teaching how the Bible can come alive for specific situations we face today. Dr. Harold Songer, retired Provost and Professor of New Testament at Southern Baptist Theological Seminary, introduced me to a broad range of effective tools for Bible study, with a major emphasis on crawling inside the thinking, emotions, practices, understandings, and situations of the culture of Bible days and then set me on the pathway of asking the correct questions of the text—what were those people going through, what did God want this text to do for and through those people, and how can that text do the same for and through us who live with computers, airplanes, high-tech, pluralism, addictions, etc.?

But this particular book would never be in your hands were it not for Jonathan Underwood, editor of adult products at the Standard Publishing Company. Jon is a keen scholar and communicator who did the unbelievable. He took a former book of mine of thirteen chapters and then rearranged, condensed, and surrounded some of the insights from that book with his outstanding comments and direction. This book has the potency to change your life, but it would not be in your hands were it not for the matchless expertise of Jon Underwood.

To him I am greatly indebted as a yoke fellow in making this tool available to you.

Knofel Staton
Fullerton, California
April 27, 1993

Introduction

Why Study the Bible?

Is it really worth taking the time to study the Bible? The answer to that question depends upon your answer to this question: "Is God worth listening to?"

The Bible is God's way of unveiling the truth for us—truth that we would not know without his sharing it with us. God has pulled back the curtain for us to see the truth about our past history, our present condition, and our future.

There is much that man can discover on his own. For instance, we can learn much about nature by observation. But there is much we could never uncover by ourselves. We would never have stumbled on the truth of how nature began without God's special communication. God pulled back the veil and showed us that "in the beginning God created the heavens and the earth" (Genesis 1:1).

We could learn from secular history that a man named Jesus from Nazareth was crucified. But without God's communication, we could never know that Christ died for our sins and saves us.

The Bible does not tell us everything about everything. But it does tell us what we need to know about God, about ourselves, and about how we can have an abundant life here on earth and an eternal life in Heaven.

Communication and Community

Communication and *community* are very important words and are related to one another. The word *community* comes from two other words, *common* and *unity*. It means the state of common oneness. Communication is the process needed to get and to stay in a state of common oneness (community).

Two people can never enter into a real community-like relationship (such as marriage) without communication, for communication is necessary if two people are really to get to know each other. By knowing one another, they can draw together into a common oneness.

I cannot know you unless I know your thoughts. And I cannot know your thoughts unless you show them to me—that's communication.

How can you show me your thoughts? You do it in two ways: (1) by what you do and (2) by what you say. Your actions and your words reveal to me who you are and what you think. If you leave one of these ways out, I will probably misunderstand you. You can tell me you love me, but if you do nothing to show me you love me, I may not believe your words. Your actions should demonstrate what you say.

On the other hand, if I look only at your actions, I may interpret them wrongly. For example, a child who has been punished by his mother may think that she does not love him any more. He needs to hear from his mother why she punished him: because she loves him and wants him to grow up to be good. He needs her actions to be interpreted by her words.

We need to understand each other and to draw closer together in a community. Communication is the means to make a community possible.

God is a person. The only way we can know him is to know his thoughts. But we cannot know his thoughts unless he chooses to show them to us through his words and actions. He has chosen to do so and has given us the Bible. The Bible is a record of God's actions and words. Through that record, we can come to know God and enjoy a common oneness with him.

The Purpose of the Bible

God has not given us the Bible so we can win Bible Bowl contests or become specialists in knowing all about it. He wants us to know about *him*. He wants us to become united to *him*. If we know the Bible, but our characters aren't being transformed into God's likeness—then we have flunked the course.

The entire Bible (both testaments) is given to direct us to Jesus, in whom we are to be re-created into the image of God, in whom we are to be re-united with God. The Bible helps us to grow into being and acting like God.

The Law

In Galatians 3:24, Paul made it clear that "the Law has become our tutor . . ." (NASB). The word *tutor* is from a Greek word that literally means a child leader. It refers to a slave who had the responsibility of leading school-age children to their teachers. This was necessary so the children would not wander off or get to the wrong teacher. The tutor's task was somewhat like that of the school-bus driver of today.

The law had that kind of responsibility. Its job was to get us lined up with the correct teacher. But who is that teacher? Note the rest of Galatians 3:24: "to lead us to Christ, that we may be justified by faith." The law points us to Jesus.

When we are in Jesus, we are no longer under the law. We no longer need the tutor (or the school-bus driver), for we have reached the right teacher. "But now that faith has come, we are no longer under a tutor" (Galatians 3:25, NASB).

The Psalms and the Prophets

The psalms and the prophets also pointed to Jesus. The prophets spotlighted his coming and informed the people what Christ would be like. Many of the psalms spoke directly about the coming Messiah (two hundred references to psalms are found in the New Testament).

The Old Testament is important to the Christian. It was the preaching of the Old Testament that convinced many people in the first century that Jesus was the Messiah (Acts 17:2, 3). The history of the Old Testament gives important examples of God's dealing with man— examples that help us in living and help us to know God's thoughts (1 Corinthians 10:1-13). The Christian must study the Old Testament to know about God and become more like him.

But is the Old Testament really the Word of God? Yes, indeed! God spoke verbally to people and then commanded them to write down what he had spoken. But how do we know that the written words we have were the spoken words of God? For one thing, God certified the writers by signs and wonders. For another, there were many people alive who heard Moses and the other Old Testament writers speak and who were also alive to read what they wrote. If there had been any discrepancies between the spoken and written words, they would have been readily evident to the people.

Much of what was spoken and written was difficult for the people to live out in their daily lives. If anything was changed, they certainly would have left out those tough sections!

The Jews had learned not to change the Word of God. Once God told the people to put all the captured silver, gold, and articles of bronze and iron into the treasury of the Lord. But in practice Achan changed the word *all* to *some* and kept some for himself. The entire nation was punished for that action (Joshua 6:15—7:26). The Jews learned not to tamper with God's Word.

The New Testament

The four Gospels—Matthew, Mark, Luke, and John— record the actions and words of Jesus, which are the actions and words of God. Jesus spoke nothing on his own initiative, only what he heard from the Father (John 12:49). Jesus did what he knew the Father would do (John 5:19), so Jesus could say, "Anyone who has seen me has seen the Father" (John 14:9).

But can we trust what we read in these four books? Perhaps people changed the content? Not at all! There were many witnesses still alive when the books were written. If there had been errors or changes, the witnesses of the happenings would have said so.

If anything was changed, why didn't they make Jesus' teachings easier to live out? Why didn't they make some of the miracles more believable? Why not cover up the cowardly conduct of the disciples on the night Jesus was betrayed?

Most of the apostles were killed (probably all but one) for their faith. It would be one thing for them to die for what they believed was the truth, but quite another for them to die for a lie that they themselves had made up.

No one denied the facts about Jesus that the apostles preached in the book of Acts. The people did not deny that Jesus arose from the dead, because many of them saw him. The disciples saw him, spoke with him, and touched him; they were not gullible or easily deceived.

The church began in the city where many of Jesus' sayings and actions had happened. The events could have been checked out easily, yet the number of disciples in the church increased and multiplied by the thousands. They would not have become part of a church that they knew was based on a fabrication. Even priests became followers of Jesus. They were the scholars who knew how to check out the truth of teachings. They knew they would lose the security of their status if they believed, but they believed.

What about the rest of the New Testament? Is it the Word of God? Oh, yes! The apostles and prophets of the New Testament were inspired to speak (John 16:13; 1 Corinthians 2:12, 13), and what they spoke was called "the word of God" (1 Thessalonians 2:13). God also certified what they spoke by signs and wonders (Acts 14:3; Romans 15:18, 19; 2 Corinthians 12:12; Hebrews 2:1-4). And what they wrote was called "Scripture" (2 Peter 3:15, 16). Therefore, what they spoke and what they wrote became the foundation upon which we are to build our lives (Ephesians 2:20).

But couldn't their writings have been changed through the centuries? Yes, they could have been. In fact, some of the manuscripts do have changes in them. But we have enough manuscripts to investigate so that we can know what changes were made.

There is no other piece of ancient literature whose accuracy we can affirm as confidently as that of the Bible. Many Old Testament manuscripts were found in caves near the Dead Sea in 1947. They show that the Old Testament we have is virtually without error. There are a few differences in spelling and word order, but not in meaning.

We have approximately five thousand manuscripts with all or parts of the New Testament on them. That allows us to do a lot of checking.

It is possible to get a PhD degree in classic literature from a university. However, the original manuscripts of all the classics have been lost, and the oldest manuscript of a copy is approximately five hundred to a thousand years later than the original—but the accuracy of that ancient literature is not challenged. We have only one manuscript of Tacitus' *Annals* and *Greek Anthology*, ten of Caesar's *Gallic War*, and only eight of the *History of Thucydides*. None of these copies is dated close to the time the original was written, yet we believe them. Evidence for the New Testament is much better.

As we read the Bible, we can trust that we are reading the Word of God. The words were not changed by the early hearers, and the original meanings have not been altered.

The Focal Point

In the Bible, God communicates his thoughts so we can know him. To know him is to love him, and to love him is to serve him. But serving begins by believing in Jesus. Jesus is the focal point of the whole Bible.

The Old Testament points to his coming. The Gospels reveal his actions and speech when he did come. Acts traces the history of how his disciples crossed all human barriers to tell of his life and mission. All the teachings in the letters to individuals and churches are based upon the teachings of Jesus and show us how we can mature toward becoming like Jesus. The book of Revelation declares that the ones in Jesus are victorious, regardless of the earthly opposition they may face.

The Bible moves from a garden, where man was created and lived in complete harmony with God, to a city, where man will once again be in complete harmony with God. The Old Testament declares, "Jesus is coming." The New Testament declares, "Jesus was here and is coming again." The final words in the Bible prepare us for that coming: "'Yes, I am coming soon.' Amen. Come, Lord Jesus!" (Revelation 22:20).

The Bible is God's communication to us. It is worth studying—if having an eternal community-like relationship with God is worth having. Is it worth it to you? If it is, then there is one conclusion you cannot escape:

You Must Study the Bible

The Bible is recognized worldwide as a great book of history and literature. It has been on the best-seller list for years. Yet there are multitudes of people who do not know what the Bible means.

There are many opinions about the Bible, many interpretations of it. How can we sift through them all and find the truth? Why do people disagree about what the Bible says? The reason does not lie in the Bible itself, but in the readers. It is nothing new for students to see the Bible differently.

Tradition Versus the Bible

In Jesus' day the Jews were divided into various groups. Each group had a different slant on what the Bible said and meant. The Pharisees would not let the written Word be enough. They educated scholars who interpreted the Word with such fine-tuned applications that the people quoted the scholars as much as they quoted the written Word of God, and perhaps more.

To speak with "authority" was to say, "Rabbi So-and-so said." The longer this went on, the more Bible study was left for the scholars. The non-scholarly member was off the hook. He would let the scholars study the written Word for him. The applications and interpretations of the scholars became the authoritative Word. People merely passed on what they were taught without doing their own study.

The interpretations and applications that were passed on from generation to generation became known as the "traditions of the elders." People thought, "If it's good enough for the elders, the spiritual leaders among us, then it's good enough for us."

A person's spirituality was evaluated by how well he or she observed the "traditions of the elders" rather than the written Word. On one occasion, the Pharisees put a judgmental question to Jesus: "Why do your disciples break the tradition of the elders? They don't wash their hands before they eat" (Matthew 15:2).

Jesus did not let that question rattle him. He was determined not to allow tradition to ride shotgun over the written Word of God. He returned the question as if it were a stinging boomerang: "And why do you break the command of God for the sake of your tradition?" (Matthew 15:3).

Jesus continued to outline how they had failed to apply God's commandment to honor their fathers and mothers. He called them hypocrites because their lips honored God, but their hearts were far away from him (Matthew 15:8). They were teaching the traditions of men as God's will instead of teaching the Word of God (Matthew 15:9).

It is entirely possible to honor God with our lips and worship him regularly and still be hypocrites because we teach man's conclusions rather than God's commandments. How about you? Have you ever communicated "traditions" of men rather than the commandments of God? I find it is easy to do, and I confess that I have done it many times.

Just for fun, take this test. Put a *B* beside each statement that is made in the Bible, and an *X* beside each one that is not.

___ 1. To miss the Lord's Supper is to sin.
___ 2. Tithing is commanded in the New Testament.
___ 3. The Christian is commanded to keep the Ten Commandments.
___ 4. The Lord's Supper has to be observed on Sunday only.
___ 5. Baptism has nothing to do with salvation.
___ 6. The Lord's Supper must be observed by the church every week.
___ 7. Baptism is sprinkling or pouring.
___ 8. Acts 6 tells how the first deacons were selected.

___ 9. The New Testament Christian does not need to study the Old Testament.

___ 10. Deacons have to handle the finances in the church, while the elders have to handle the spiritual matters.

___ 11. Only deacons and elders may serve the Lord's Supper.

___ 12. Only elders are to pray at the Lord's table.

___ 13. An invitation hymn must be sung at the end of every worship service.

___ 14. A Christian must speak in tongues.

___ 15. Benevolence is not a necessary activity of the church.

___ 16. Congregations must be totally independent of each other.

___ 17. The Bible gives a set pattern for worship services.

___ 18. The method of supporting missionaries is clearly outlined in the Bible.

___ 19. Baptisms must be on Sunday.

___ 20. There is only one good version of the Bible.

___ 21. A Christian must not have non-Christian friends.

___ 22. There is no place for religion in politics.

___ 23. Only paid preachers are to be considered ministers.

___ 24. There is no biblical command to pay preachers.

___ 25. It is wrong for anyone to wear robes in the worship service.

All of the above statements should be marked with an *X*, for none is clearly made in the Bible. That does not mean that all of them are false. We may consider some of them reasonable and proper; but we have no right to force them upon others, because the Bible does not state them plainly.

Prejudice Versus the Bible

Not only is it possible to substitute tradition for what the Bible says and means, but it also is possible to be blinded to biblical truth because of prejudicial teachings. The Jews in Jesus' day were trapped in that way. Their teachers had handled the Old Testament prophecies about the coming Messiah as if they were being treated to a smorgasbord meal. They had picked out the prophecies they liked and rejected the ones they didn't like.

They liked the prophecy that the Messiah would sit on David's throne forevermore. They liked to read, "Of the increase of his government and peace there will be no end" (Isaiah 9:7). They stressed *forevermore* and concluded that when the Messiah came, he would live forever. But what about those passages that spoke about the death of the Messiah? The teachers concluded they must be referring to someone else.

An Ethiopian returning home after worshiping at Jerusalem was reading one such prophecy:

> He was led like a sheep to the slaughter;
> And as a lamb before the shearer is silent,
> So he did not open his mouth.
> In his humiliation he was deprived of justice.
> Who can speak of his descendants?
> For his life was taken from the earth (Acts 8:32, 33).

The reader did not know he was reading a messianic prophecy. He wondered if the prophet might be speaking of himself (Acts 8:34).

One time after Jesus taught the people that he would die, the multitude responded, "We have heard from the Law that the Christ will remain forever, so how can you say, 'The Son of Man must be lifted up'?" (John 12:34). A crowd of people was telling Jesus he was wrong. Their problem was that they had not studied the Law for themselves. They had just "heard."

What about you? Do you decide what you believe about certain issues without studying the Bible to see what it says? If so, you need this book.

One of the greatest compliments paid to any Jews in the New Testament was given to the Jews in Berea. They "examined the Scriptures every day to see if what Paul said was true" (Acts 17:11). The Jews in Thessalonica did not do so. They already had their minds made up, so they created

15

a mob of violence when Paul preached a message that did not square with their prejudices (Acts 17:5). Yes, it is much easier to oppose a teaching than to study for the truth.

It also is possible to ignore some of the major doctrinal teachings of the Bible because of lack of study. The Sadducees were guilty of this. They did not believe in a resurrection because they were led to believe that it wasn't taught in the Bible.

Jesus did not excuse them with, "I'm sorry your teachers misled you." Oh, no! He put the responsibility of knowing the truth on their shoulders. "Is this not the reason you are mistaken, that you do not understand the Scriptures, or the power of God?" (Mark 12:24, NASB).

Can you begin to see the tragedies that result when God's people do not study the Word of God? Such tragedies are numerous:

1. People divide into various groups that rest upon the teachings of certain leaders. They elevate traditions of men to a place equal with God's Word. They may ignore some of the major doctrines in the Bible. They may even miss the true Messiah and still be looking for him.

2. In recent years many young people who were raised in the church have been taken in by a variety of pseudo-messiahs and their cults.

3. People who have spent eighteen years in our worship services and Sunday-school classes reject the Bible and God after one semester on a university campus.

4. Others who have spent thirty years in Sunday school and church claim that they do not know enough to teach others. Isn't it odd that a person with four years of Bible college (about a thousand hours in Bible-related classes) is considered to be more knowledgeable about the Bible than a person who has spent three thousand hours in thirty years of Sunday school and church services?

When God's Word is not known, people will turn to other sources for help to cope with life. Some will turn inward to dreams, inner voices, and ESP; others will turn outward to astrology, witchcraft, and the occult. Any nation that is not equipped with a knowledge and application of God's Word will degenerate in morals and will eventually disintegrate as a nation. People cannot handle well the complexities of life without God's guidance. They need help from the written Word of God. But it must be studied by everyone. When it isn't, trouble multiplies.

Why should you study the Bible? Because you will be in error if you do not understand it (Matthew 22:29). Because it was written for your guidance (Psalm 119:105). Because it was inspired by God (2 Peter 1:20, 21). Because you are to speak the truth (Ephesians 4:15); how can you speak the truth unless you know it? Because you and other Christians are to reach a unity in faith and knowledge (Ephesians 4:13). Because the Holy Spirit works through the written Word (Ephesians 6:17).

You are to keep God's commands (1 John 5:3); how can you if you do not know them? You must study the Bible because Christ wants his words to abide in you (John 15:7). You will be judged in the last day by God's Word, not by words of men (John 12:48). You are to handle accurately "the word of truth" (2 Timothy 2:15); how can you without study? The Scriptures help mature you (2 Timothy 3:16, 17). God will bless you if you observe his Word (Luke 11:28). You must increase in knowledge, wisdom, and understanding (Colossians 1:9, 10); you cannot grow in this way without study of God's Word.

A Time Problem?

Do you have time to devote to study? Of course you do. The real question is, how do you use the time you have? For nearly twenty years, leisure-time activities have been the nation's number one industry. Why? Because Americans have *much* leisure time.

In his book, *Religion and Leisure in America*, Robert Lee points out that leisure time should not be "a vacation from reality." It is a time for countless helpful and pleasant activities. Mr. Lee lists some of them as follows:

A time of discovery.
A time for learning and freedom.
A time of growth and expression.
A time for rest and restoration.
A time for discovering life in its wholeness.

To get the most out of this book and out of the Bible, you will have to commit some of your leisure time to the discovery that comes from Bible study. Fill in the following chart with the number of hours in a week you spend on each of the following activities:

Activity	Hours Spent per Week
Preparing for work	
On the job	
Preparing meals	
Eating	
Housework	
Doing laundry	
Attending meetings	
Shopping	
Running errands	
Yard work and odd jobs	
Sleeping	
Other	

Now add up the total hours (add other categories if needed) and subtract from 168. The answer will be the number of leisure hours you have. How are you using them? Surely there is some time for Bible study! God's Word is worth some of that time, isn't it?

But *how* can you study it? That is the reason we have this book. It is a book for you. It is to be like a map, guiding you into territory that may be strange but will be enjoyable. You will need a pen or pencil, paper, and a Bible. Have a happy journey!

Step One

Getting Ready

An Overview of Bible Study

As we study the Bible, there are three steps we must take: *observe, interpret,* and *apply.* These steps are not different or unusual. In fact, I venture a guess that you take the same steps in other matters every day of your life. Let me illustrate.

My family and I used to live in one of the tornado alleys of the nation. Sirens had been installed to warn the residents when a tornado had been sighted. But that was not the only time the sirens were blown. Therefore, whenever I observed that the sirens were blowing, I had to interpret what I was observing and respond, or apply what I had learned, appropriately.

To *interpret* is simply to tell the meaning. When I observed the sound of the sirens, I had to ask what that sound meant. To determine its meaning, I would look at the surrounding situation. If I saw a beautiful clear sky, I knew that no tornado had been sighted. Then I considered the other possibilities: (1) Was it noon? (2) Was it a civil defense test? (3) Was there an electrical short in the siren? My answer to these questions determined my interpretation.

After I had investigated and interpreted the sound, I made an application. If it was stormy, I headed for the basement. If it was noon, I ate. If it was a civil defense test, I continued with what I was doing before I heard the sirens.

You take these steps many times a day. Suppose you observe someone winking at you. You consider the situation and interpret the meaning of that wink as one of the following: (1) He likes you. (2) She is making fun of what someone else is doing or saying. (3) He is saying, "I'm kidding." (4) She has dust in her eyes. (5) He has a twitch in his eyelid. Then you respond (make application) accordingly.

It is possible to goof in our interpretations. Suddenly you observe a red flashing light on the car behind you. You interpret its meaning: "It's the police and he's after me!" So you make application and pull over to the curb. But the police car just keeps on going. Your interpretation was wrong—he was after the fellow ahead of you.

You observe that one of your friends hasn't called you in several days. You interpret the meaning: she is angry with you. You make application and decide you won't call her either. But a week later you find that your interpretation was wrong. Your friend was sick in bed.

Observation

The moment you begin to read the Bible, you are taking the first step in Bible study (observation). You note the letters, the words, the sentences, and the paragraphs. It is important to observe carefully. You don't want to miss anything.

Evaluate your past observations of Scripture by marking each of these statements with a T for true or an F for false.

___ 1. The Bible says Eve sinned by eating an apple.
___ 2. On the night Jesus was born, the Bible says, angels sang to shepherds in nearby fields.
___ 3. Three wise men came to the manger to see the baby Jesus.
___ 4. When Jesus ascended into heaven, the Bible says the angels told the apostles that he would return.
___ 5. Coming to the tomb of Jesus, Mary Magdalene saw two angels sitting outside the open doorway.
___ 6. Saul's name was changed to Paul at his conversion.

All the answers are false. How observant have you been? (1) "Apple" is not mentioned, just "fruit" (Genesis 3:6). (2) Luke 2:13 says the angels were "praising God and saying." What they said is poetic, and many of us conclude they sang; but this is interpretation. (3) The number of wise men is not mentioned, and they came to a "house," not to a "manger" (Matthew 2:1-11). (4) The Bible says two "men" spoke to the apostles (Acts 1:10). Their white clothing and their message make us think they were angels, but this is interpretation. (5) The angels were inside the tomb (John 20:12); (6) Saul was still called Saul after his conversion (Acts 9:22, 24; 11:25, 30; 12:25; 13:1, 2, 7, 9). Probably he had two names from birth, but began to use his Roman-Greek name, "Paul," as he traveled among Gentiles.

Faulty observation is easier than you thought, isn't it?

A program of Bible reading. It is important that you begin a systematic and regular program of Bible reading. You can never hope to interpret the meaning of the Bible correctly or hope to apply the teachings of the Bible to your daily life unless you take this first step of careful and regular Bible reading.

I am suggesting a way that you can read through the New Testament once every two months, the book of Psalms every four months, the book of Proverbs once a month, and the rest of the Old Testament twice a year. Here is the plan:

1. Divide the number of pages in your New Testament by 60. The answer is the number of pages of the New Testament you should read every day.
2. Read one chapter of Proverbs every day.
3. Read one Psalm every day.
4. Subtract the number of pages of Psalms and Proverbs from the number of pages in your Old Testament. Divide the remainder by 180. Your resulting number will be the number of pages of the Old Testament you should read every day.

Is this too much time to spend reading the Bible? Before you answer, check again how much leisure time you have. You will be surprised at how rapidly this way of reading the Bible will enable you to see relationships and get a grasp of what God is saying.

To get the most out of your reading, keep a notebook close at hand and jot down words that you don't understand, questions that come to mind, things you want to investigate, and how each Scripture applies to you.

Interpretation

If the Bible is the Word of God, why do we have to interpret it? If we interpret it, aren't we changing it? No, not necessarily. As I have already illustrated, interpretation is natural and necessary.

Translations. The moment you pick up a Bible, you are picking up an interpretation of it. When a person translates words from one language into another, interpretation plays a part. One foreign word often can be translated into any of several English words; therefore, a translator must decide which English word best transfers the meaning the writer intended when he used the foreign word. He has to decide what word the writer would have used to convey the same meaning if he were to have written in English.

Also, at the time the Bible was written, there were no punctuation marks to indicate the ends of sentences or paragraphs. There were no verse numbers or chapter divisions. The writers did not even put spaces between the words. Therefore, the readers and translators of the ancient manuscripts had to decide where to space between words and where to end sentences and paragraphs.

To better understand the problem, try to make sense out of the following: GODISNOWHERE. What does it say? You have three choices: (1) a bunch of letters that make no sense, (2) GOD IS NOWHERE, (3) GOD IS NOW HERE. There is a world of difference in these choices, and where you place the spaces makes the difference.

Transferring meaning from the old manuscripts was a tough job. We should be thankful for the people who did so. It would be awful for us to have to read the Old Testament in Hebrew and the New Testament in Greek, wouldn't it? And don't let the fact of translating disturb you. Translators were not trying to mislead us; they were trying to help us. We can check their work by comparing the various versions. (See the second half of this chapter.)

Determine the meaning. To determine the meaning of a passage: (1) Determine who is writing. (2) Note to whom it is written. (3) Read the verses directly before and after the passage to determine the literary context. (4) Determine the cultural context—the situation in the lives of the first readers. (5) Determine the meaning of the words. (6) Investigate what other Scriptures say about the issue or topic. Filling out an outline in a notebook may be helpful. (See the example at the top of the next page.)

Application

Determining what the writer intended his words to mean to his first readers will help you to be able to understand

---
Outline Format

Text: _____

To whom is it written? _____

Do I fit into the same category? _____

Truths in this passage: _____

_____

Words I need to study: _____

_____

What I learn from the context (verses before and after):

_____

What is the setting (situation of first readers)? _____

_____

What do other Scriptures say about this issue? _____

_____

---

what those same words mean to you. It is especially important to discern to whom the Scripture is written and if it then applies to you. Some promises and commands were given to certain people at certain times, but are not meant for you.

For instance, Jesus was speaking to his apostles when he said, "But the Helper, the Holy Spirit, whom the Father will send in My name, He will teach you all things, and bring to your remembrance all that I said to you" (John 14:26, NASB). That promise is not meant for you because you are not an apostle. You were not with Jesus when he was on earth, and so you cannot be an eyewitness as the apostles were (John 15:27). You can have the Holy Spirit living within you and helping you (Acts 2:38; 1 Corinthians 6:19), but you cannot expect the same unfailing inspiration the apostles had.

An Exercise

Before reading any further, try out what you have just learned. Read the first chapter of Ephesians and note every blessing that comes through Jesus. Then determine the following:

1. Who wrote it?

2. To whom was it written?

3. Do you fit into the same category?

Can you find any application for you in this chapter? Here are some questions to help you:

A. If the church is Christ's body, what are you?

B. What are the functions of your body?

C. Then what are the functions of Christ's body?

D. In what specific ways can you personally help the body of Christ function?

Tools for Bible Study

Studying the Word of God by observing, interpreting, and applying is essential and exciting, but it is not easy. It takes thought and time. It cannot be done during the television commercials, but it can be done by anyone who can read. There is no need to feel all alone or at a loss as to how to go about it. Many tools are available to help you.

I encourage you to purchase at least one tool each month until the most useful ones are in your personal library. Within a year you can have the basic tools. These tools are not essential, but they are very helpful. They will save you time and add direction to your study. They will help you avoid that feeling of frustration that comes from not knowing how to go about solving a problem in Bible study.

Versions or Translations

It is helpful to have several good versions of the Bible: King James Version (KJV), American Standard Version (ASV), Revised Standard Version (RSV), New American Standard Bible (NASB), Jerusalem Bible (JB), New International Version (NIV), Today's English Version (TEV), the New Century Version (NCV; also known as the International Children's Bible), the New Revised Standard Version (NRSV), the Contemporary English Version (CEV), and others. You can find them in your religious bookstore.

Why do we have so many different versions? I can see that it must be confusing. A person may wonder, "Which one should I use?" or, "Why can't the Christian world settle on one version?" But the many different versions can actually make Bible study easier and understanding more accurate.

Since the Old Testament was originally written in Hebrew and the New Testament in Greek, translations are necessary for English readers. But some groups of people do not respond as well to one style of English as they do to another, and so there are different versions. These versions use different words and different styles, but the meaning is essentially the same. I can understand a modern version better, but my grandmother prefers a version in the language style to which she is accustomed.

Also, over a long period of history, words change in meaning. A version prepared three hundred years ago uses words that are not used in the same way or have the same meaning today.

Comparing different versions of a passage of Scripture can help us in determining the meaning of words. It is possible to purchase a Bible that has six different versions printed side by side in columns. You may find this extremely helpful and not as cumbersome as six different Bibles would be.

For your guidance, here is a brief description of some of the more popular English versions of the Bible.

King James Version. This is an excellent version, but it uses approximately four hundred English words that are no longer used in common communication. It also has many English words whose meanings have changed in the past three hundred fifty years. For example, *conversation* used to mean conduct, but we use it today to mean speech. If we did not know this, we would think James was referring to talk when he said, "Let him show out of a good conversation his works" (James 3:13).

The word *let* used to mean hinder. Paul wrote, "Now I would not have you ignorant, brethren, that oftentimes I purposed to come unto you, (but was let hitherto)" (Romans 1:13). Reading that today, a person might think that Paul was allowed to go to Rome, but Paul was really saying he had been prevented from going.

Consulting modern versions can help us eliminate such mistaken understandings. For example, what does *importunity* mean in the King James Version of Luke 11:8? I heard a Sunday school teacher pronounce the word as "importanty" and proceed to say that the church should do whatever important people in the community tell it to do, as the neighbor in this parable did for the important man. It was abundantly clear that the teacher did not know the meaning of the word *importunity*. If he had consulted a modern version, he would have discovered that the word means persistence.

Some may ask, "Why don't we just use an English dictionary instead of consulting the various versions?" That would help in many cases. But who will stop to look up a word like *conversation* when he already knows its meaning? Unfortunately the meaning he knows is not the one James had in mind. A modern version informs the reader of the true meaning by translating *behavior* instead of *conversation*. An English dictionary gives both the old meaning of the word and the new meaning, but a modern version lets us know which one Jesus had in mind.

American Standard Version. A revision of the King James Version was completed in 1881 in Great Britain, the

Revised Version. A group of American scholars on the revision committee had favored a number of alternate readings that were not accepted. These scholars in turn produced the ASV in 1901. It updates many of the outdated words and is a good, literal translation.

Revised Standard Version/New Revised Standard Version. The RSV was a revision of the American Standard Version, completed in 1952. The NRSV, another revision, appeared in 1990.

New American Standard Bible. This 1971 revision of the ASV is an excellent translation, depending heavily on the Greek and Hebrew and not merely updating the older English work.

The Jerusalem Bible. This version was done by Catholic scholars and is a fresh, excellent work.

Today's English Version. This version is in understandable language and often uses British terminology.

The Cottonpatch Version. The late Clarence Jordan produced this cross-cultural version of the New Testament to portray the emotional nuances of the Greek in contemporary southern U.S. dialog.

The New Testament in the Language of the People. This is a very important translation of the New Testament. Charles B. Williams handles the Greek verb tenses in a helpful way.

New International Version. This translation has aimed for clarity, simplicity, and accuracy. It does a good job of explaining some of the cultural terms. For instance, a *denarius* is referred to as a "day's pay," which allows us to understand its value.

New King James Version. The Thomas Nelson company introduced this revision in 1982. It updates most of the archaic vocabulary of the KJV, but strives to maintain its poetic beauty.

International Children's Bible/New Century Version. This version calls itself the "first translation of the Holy Scriptures prepared specifically for children." Not a paraphrase or storybook Bible, the ICB was translated on a third-grade instructional level.

Contemporary English Version. Currently available only in the New Testament, the American Bible Society is producing this work to speak the language of today.

A very helpful addition to this line is a parallel Bible or New Testament. This kind of tool lists several versions of most verses so you can compare how a variety of versions translates a single text. Curtis Vaughn's *Twenty-six Translations of the Bible* is undoubtedly the most comprehensive.

Paraphrase

Another important tool is a paraphrase of the Bible. Often it helps us understand the intention of the writers. A paraphrase is not a close translation of the original language, but an attempt to put its meaning in language easy to understand. Sometimes a paraphrase can be misleading because it is less accurate than a translation, but usually it is excitingly enlightening. Two popular ones are *The New Testament in Modern English,* by J. B. Phillips, and *The Living Bible.*

Concordance

An exhaustive concordance lists in alphabetical order every major word used in the Bible, and lists every place that word appears in the Bible. It is a gold mine of information. In a later chapter, I will show you how to use one most beneficially. The two best ones are Robert Young's *Analytical Concordance to the Bible* and James Strong's *Exhaustive Concordance of the Bible.* You can buy these at any religious bookstore or at the bookstore in the Bible college near you. You may find you can use one at the public library or the church library. Perhaps you will prefer to buy a less expensive and less complete book to begin with, like *Cruden's Complete Concordance.* Usually it will help you in finding a passage; and when it doesn't, you can go to the library. In addition to these works, keyed to the King James version, complete or exhaustive concordances to the NIV and NASB are also available

Bible Dictionary

A Bible dictionary does much more than give the meanings of words. It is more like an encyclopedia that gives information about the major topics of the Bible. The topics and words are listed alphabetically. You can purchase a one-volume dictionary or a comprehensive multi-volume encyclopedia. At first, the one-volume kind may be sufficient. Two good ones are *Zondervan's Pictorial Bible Dictionary* and *The New Bible Dictionary*. If you are ready for a multi-volume one, you will like *Zondervan's Pictorial Encyclopedia of the Bible* or the *New International Bible Encyclopedia*. A classic work that has recently been updated in a most helpful way is the *International Standard Bible Encyclopedia*.

A Word Book

In addition to a concordance and a Bible dictionary, there are other good tools for finding the meaning of words: William Barclay's *New Testament Words* and *More New Testament Words*, Alan Richardson's *A Theological Word Book of the Bible*, and Vine, Unger, and White's *Expository Dictionary of Biblical Words*.

Books on the Cultural Background

The Bible comes alive when you know the setting and situation of a story or a teaching. For example, did you know a Jewish man could divorce his wife if she talked to another man? Or did you know the Hebrews' fall thanksgiving festival lasted a week instead of a day? While some such information can be gleaned from a Bible dictionary, much more can be discovered in books such as these: Daniel-Rops' *Daily Life in the Time of Jesus*, Alfred Edersheim's *The Life and Times of Jesus the Messiah*, Joachim Jeremias' *Jerusalem in the Time of Jesus*, and Charles Guignebert's *The Jewish World in the Time of Jesus*.

Maps or Bible Atlas

Information about the geography of Bible times can help a great deal to orient us as we read about various locations in the Bible. With a good map beside you, you won't be reading about vague places and events. You will be able to picture events and trace the journeys more easily. You may find enough maps in the back of a good Bible, along with an index for finding places. In addition to maps, a good Bible atlas provides important information, history, Scripture references, and pictures of places. Three good ones are *Rand McNally Bible Atlas, Oxford Bible Atlas,* and the recent *NIV Atlas of the Bible.* Standard Publishing also has a very good inexpensive atlas, the *Standard Bible Atlas.*

Use the Tools

As soon as you buy each tool, get acquainted with it, practice using it, and discover its possibilities. Using the concordance and dictionary, look up topics and words that you always have wondered about. Use a different Bible version in Sunday school class and the worship services. Compare the different wording in familiar passages. You will be surprised at the new thoughts that will come to you.

Read a book on the cultural background of the first century, relating the new information to familiar New Testament teachings. The Bible will come alive for you. Read through a small New Testament book in a paraphrase and see how enjoyable it is. Follow the missionary journeys of Paul on the maps and read about each city in a Bible dictionary. You will be amazed at how much more interesting the journeys become.

Summary

As carpentry tools are important for building a house quickly and accurately, so Bible-study tools are important for building our lives upon the foundation of God's Word.

The proper use of these tools will prevent us from allowing our prejudices to dictate our understanding of what the Bible means.

There is an interesting story of two men who were participants in a week-long tree-cutting contest. One man began cutting trees at five in the morning and quit at five in the evening each day. The second man did not even go to the woods until the third day, and then he cut trees from nine in the morning until three in the afternoon.

At the end of the week, the second man had cut more trees than the first man. When he was asked how he could do it in less time, the second man replied, "That's simple. While he was out cutting trees the first two days, I was sharpening my axe."

Questions for Discussion

1. Which is the hardest step in Bible study: observing, interpreting, or applying? Why?
2. Look at the true-or-false quiz the author supplies under the heading, "Observation." Did you know every statement was false? Why is it so easy to make a mistake on these statements?
3. If you have not completed the exercise the author suggests, do so now. Compare your results with another person's. Are they basically the same? If there are differences, did someone fail to observe carefully? If your interpretations differ, who is right? How can you tell?
4. What tools for Bible study do you own? What tools are available in your church library? What tools would you like to add to your own library?
5. What Bible versions have you used? Which one or two do you prefer? Why?

Step Two

Reading for Meaning

I want you to be sure of one thing: *You can understand the Bible.* I am afraid many people neglect God's Word because they are programmed to believe they cannot understand it. I must admit that some of the sermons and Sunday school lessons I have heard are complex and unorganized enough to give the impression that the Bible is unintelligible to all but an enlightened few. In truth, understanding the Bible may be a bit difficult, but you *can* do it.

God intended that everyone be able to understand his communication. Paul wrote some of his letters to immature Christians—people who had not been Christians very long. They had not spent years in Sunday school classes as many of us have. The two letters to Thessalonians were written to a group of people who were only a few months old in the Christian faith; the two letters to Corinthians went to those who had been in Christ only a few years. Paul had to write to them as "infants in Christ" (1 Corinthians 3:1, 2).

The Bible was written for people much like you and me. The first readers never dreamed about going to a Bible college before they attempted to understand the Bible. Paul mentioned that most of the readers God had in mind were not super-wise or well trained (1 Corinthians 1:26).

Growing Up

The Bible is like a ten-course meal: there is something for everyone. A little baby cannot handle all of such a meal, but he can handle some of it. As he matures, he can handle more. Someday his digestive system will be mature enough for the full meal.

The same is true of Christians and their relationship to the Bible. John wrote, "I am writing to you, *little children*... I am writing to you, *fathers*... I am writing to you, *young men*..." (1 John 2:12, 13, NASB). This can be applied to spiritual childhood and maturity as well as to chronological age. There is something in this short letter for new Christians (children), for the Christians who are still spiritual adolescents (young men), and for the spiritually mature persons (fathers). Whoever you are and whatever you know, God has a message for you in his Word.

But notice that John did not say, "Just read the part that applies to you." No, we are to read the whole thing, but we are not to become upset if some of it is "over our heads." Don't ever give up. Apply what you can understand to your life, and you will progress and mature from a little child to a father or mother in the faith. Each of us begins with the "milk" (1 Peter 2:2) and should advance to the stage of "solid food" (Hebrews 5:11–6:3). Children do not grow up overnight. Often they are impatient because the process is so slow. Likewise our growth in understanding the Bible may seem slow, but it is sure if we keep on studying it and applying what we learn.

Paul sharply criticized some Christians for being satisfied with baby food all the time (1 Corinthians 3:1-3). I know we would be disappointed if we still had to use baby talk with our adult children. Can't you imagine how God feels if we become self-satisfied and refuse to grow beyond his "baby talk" to us? It is time for all of us to commit ourselves to growing up.

To grow up in Christ we must *want* to know God's Word. Perhaps that is part of our problem—we do not want to know. Knowing his Word carries with it the responsibility to put it into practice in our daily lives. But learning to take responsibility is a big part of growing up, isn't it?

Mark Twain once said that it wasn't the parts of the Bible that he didn't understand that bothered him, but the parts he *did* understand. Let us seek to understand all of it; but at the same time, let us realize that the truth and meaning will dawn upon us one stage at a time as we grow in Christ.

One of the beauties of God's Word is that we never can master completely all the depth of meaning in its truths. The purpose of the Bible is to master us, and the more we read it and heed it, the more we can be mastered by it. So let's see ourselves as the kind of people God wants to understand his Word.

Principles of Reading

Marvelous treasures of truth are in the Bible, but we may fail to realize this because we have developed bad habits in our reading. The suggested program of regular reading that was outlined in Step 1 will help to keep the Word coming into your mind and eventually will enable you to see how the Bible "hangs together." But as you prepare for a lesson on a particular Scripture passage, there are some helpful principles to follow to gain the most understanding of the Word.

Determine Who Is Writing and to Whom

Is the passage written to Christians or non-Christians? Is it written to a congregation of the first century that was facing a specific situation? Whatever is written applies to the first readers first.

Some of the New Testament books do not tell us to whom they were written. Three of the Gospels—Matthew, Mark, and John—do not tell us. We can, however, assume a great deal about the readers from what the writers stress and emphasize.

Just because a letter was written to a specific person or congregation nearly two thousand years ago, we need not conclude that the letter is not speaking to us also. If the letter was written to a group of Christians and you are a Christian, then what has been written applies to you also. If you aren't a Christian, then you may need to become one before some passages will fully apply to you. Sometimes the writer singles out a particular kind of person in a congregation to teach something specifically to him or her. When this happens, you need to ask yourself if you fit into that category also. If you are a person of the same kind and in similar circumstances, the message is for you. It may be helpful even if you are not in similar circumstances. If it helps you avoid a problem, that may be better than solving it.

Most of the books in the New Testament were letters that God inspired men to write to individuals and churches to help with specific problems. Like most letters, they began with a greeting. This greeting usually revealed who was writing and to whom. When we write letters, we usually greet the person we are writing at the beginning, and then close the letter with our signature; but in the first century the writer was revealed in the greeting. Sometimes his name was also at the end. When a letter was dictated and a secretary did the actual writing, it was especially appropriate for the one who dictated it to add an ending and signature in his own handwriting as evidence that the message came from him. See the last verse of Colossians for an example.

Look at the letters named in the chart below. Determine who was writing, to whom, and whether the letter applies to you. If the author is not stated, leave a blank.

Book	To Whom	By Whom	Do I Fit?
Luke-Acts			
1 Corinthians			
Galatians			
Ephesians			
Philippians			
Colossians			
1 Thessalonians			
1 Timothy			
Titus			
Philemon			
James			
1 Peter			
Jude			
Revelation			

Now look in the letters for people who were singled out for specific instruction. For example, in Philippians 4:2, Paul singles out two women who were not getting along. Does that apply to you? It does if you are not getting along with a fellow Christian.

Notice the next verse (4:3). Paul specifies someone to help these women improve their relationship. We do not know this person, but evidently he was someone these women respected. Perhaps you are this type of person— someone who can help others get along. If so, don't sit on the sidelines; be a peacemaker.

Now consider the specific people indicated on the chart on page 38. (Make a copy twice as big as the miniature here.) Then study the references and fill out the chart.

Disregard Verse Divisions When Reading

Verse divisions were not added to the text until centuries after the New Testament was written. They sometimes

Bible Reference	Specific People	Do I Fit?	Their Responsibility	My Responsibility
1 Co. 1:10-12				
1 Co. 6:1, 7				
Eph. 5:22, 23				
Eph. 5:25-32				
Eph. 6:1, 2				
Phil. 4:1				
2 Th. 3:10-15				
1 Tim. 1:3, 4				
1 Tim. 5:4				
1 Tim. 5:17-19				
1 Pet. 5:1-4				
1 Pet. 5:5				
3 Jn. 9, 10				
Jd. 10				
Jd. 16, 19				

hinder proper Bible understanding, but they do help in locating and memorizing passages.

They are a hindrance in understanding the Bible when we begin reading Scripture at the beginning of a verse and finish reading at the end of the verse. This pulls a verse out of its context, and thus its meaning may be changed. Often that one verse is not even a complete sentence, so we are pulling words out of a sentence.

We need to read the Bible by sentences and paragraphs. If you find this difficult, try a version that divides the text into paragraphs, such as the New International Version or the New Century Version.

Make it a habit to read by starting at the beginning of a sentence and not finishing the thought until you reach the end of the sentence, no matter what the verse divisions are. A sentence ends in a period, question mark, or exclamation point. A colon or semicolon does not end a sentence. Note that everything in a sentence hangs together.

Exercise this new technique by reading Ephesians 4, noting where each sentence begins and ends, and noting the main thought of the sentence. Make an enlarged copy of this chart for your notes. If you use a version with more or less sentences than 17 (as the NASB) adjust column 1 accordingly.

Sentence Number	Begins w/ Verse	Ends w/ Verse	Main Thought
1			
2			
3			
4			
5			
6			
7			
8			
9			
10			
11			
12			
13			
14			
15			
16			
17			

If you have questions about words or topics, use the tools discussed in Step One. It is well worth the effort.

Questions for Discussion

1. Why do you think some people seem to make a deliberate effort to make others believe understanding the Bible is a special art reserved only for themselves and a few others? Do you agree that *anyone* can understand the Bible? Why or why not?

2. What do you think you should do when reading a section of Scripture that you cannot understand? Be prepared to give reasons for your answer.
   a. Don't worry about it. You must be too immature; you'll grow up some day.
   b. Just meditate on it, waiting for its meaning to dawn on you.
   c. Ask your preacher.
   d. Look up the passage in a Bible commentary.
   e. Other. Explain.

3. What do you think of Mark Twain's assessment, that it was not the parts of the Bible he did not understand that bothered him, but the parts he did understand? Do you think his attitude is typical of non-Christians today? Of Christians?

4. Complete the chart on page 36. What new insights did you discover by paying attention to who was writing and to whom?

5. Complete the chart on page 37. How many of your responses under "My Responsibility" are concepts you had not realized before? What can you do to act on these responsibilities?

6. Complete the chart on page 38. What new insights did reading sentences instead of verses provide?

Step Three

Getting the Context

Our son, Randy, played in Little League baseball as a child. He did well and had a lot of fun at it, but he would have been a total failure if he had watched the professional ball players on television and said, "I'll never be able to do that. There's no sense in trying." Randy did learn to play baseball, however, and to play pretty well. Why? Because he learned the game one step at a time. He had skilled coaches who took the time and had the patience to teach the boys at a pace they could handle.

I suspect that is the way you learned the many skills you have. Remember when you first started to drive a car? You wondered whether you would be able to remember what you had to do, and in the right order. Or remember when you first served a meal to company in your home? How you wanted to have all the food cooked and ready at the same time! Now your driving or cooking comes naturally. You don't have to be anxious about it.

It is easy to see the results of others' Bible study—the preacher, the teacher, the elder. Sometimes we are tempted to say, "I could never do that!" But stop and think. How do you think they did it? They were not born studying the Bible! They learned one step at a time. Anyone can be a good Bible student. It takes time and practice, as any skill does.

We need to help each other in Bible study, to encourage each other as members of a team do. Why not form a group and meet weekly to share the results of your Bible study?

Overview

Many people who know I used to be an air traffic controller in Chicago have asked me, "How does an air traffic controller keep all those planes straight?" Well, he doesn't walk into the control tower at the airport, grab the microphone, and begin talking to the pilots on his first day of training! He learns one step at a time. Among other things, he memorizes the whole geographical area, including the positions of landmarks, airways, and directional aids.

When studying a book of the Bible, it is essential to get an idea of the book as a whole, as a controller gets the geographical area in mind. Then you can see how the sentences and paragraphs fit together and how the meaning is developed by the author. You can never get an overview of the whole book by reading one chapter a day—unless it is a book with only one chapter! Reading just one chapter at a time chops up the thought too much. You will get some excellent and helpful ideas that way, but you will not be able to study the book in depth.

How many times have you received a many-paged letter from a friend and decided to read half a page a day just before falling to sleep at night? Ridiculous, right? Then don't read the letters from God in that way.

Read the whole book at one sitting, as you do a letter. You may be surprised to find that it takes only fifteen or twenty minutes—less than that, if it is one of the shorter books. Of course, Matthew, Luke, John, Romans, or Revelation will take longer. If you can't finish it in one sitting, do it in two—or, at the most, three—sittings instead of just reading a chapter a day.

As you read, look for the main thought, theme, or problem with which the writer is dealing. One cannot stress too much the importance of *determining the main subject of each book.* Nearly every sentence in a book relates to the theme or main subject of that book. Once you understand what point the writer is trying to drive home, you will better understand the purpose and meaning of each statement.

Don't ever pull a verse out of a book and think you know what the verse means. You may find a beautiful and inspiring thought, but you will not thoroughly understand the verse until you see it in its environment. The environment of a verse includes all of the book in which it appears.

To understand a passage of Scripture (a series of verses), we must see how the passage relates to the main topic of the book. We must *determine the situation or problem with which the writer is dealing.* We must grasp the purpose of the writer. This type of understanding is especially important if we are teaching or preaching from an assigned text. If you are using a Sunday school quarterly, you find a few verses selected for a lesson, sometimes a few verses from different books. Usually a lesson background is provided, giving enough of the setting to allow a meaningful lesson, but your own understanding will be much richer if you read the whole book.

Studying a Sunday school lesson by itself is somewhat like getting acquainted with a few streets in a town without understanding how the whole town is laid out. You usually find your way to work and back, but if you venture off the familiar route, you may become confused and fail to reach your destination. I've seen many teachers get lost in class discussions because they did not have a grasp of the purpose of the whole book. Therefore they could not confidently answer any questions or solve any problems that came up.

Whether you are a teacher or not, take time each week to read the whole book that contains the passage selected for the week's lesson. Read and reread the entire book before the lesson is presented. Be ready to share with your class the discoveries you make.

━━━━━━━━━━━━━━

Finding the Main Theme

How do you determine what is the main theme or subject of a book? You open your eyes and your mind and look for it.

Statement of Purpose

Look for any clear statement of purpose, or any clear statement of problems the book is intended to address. For example, look up John 20:30, 31. The purpose and theme of that book are plain enough, aren't they? Then look at the following passages and determine what each one tells you about the book's theme or purpose: Galatians 1:6; Colossians 2:8; 1 Timothy 1:3-5; 1 John 5:13. Sometimes you may find more than one problem clearly stated in a book. For example, see 1 Corinthians 1:10, 11; 5:1; 6:1; 7:1; 8:1; 12:1; 15:12; 16:1. If you think any one of these problems could be the theme of a book, you're right! But since all of them are in one book, make a list of them and see if you can discern one concern that runs through the solution of them all. Did you notice Paul's concern with fellowship?

Repetition of a Topic

Look for any topic or problem that is repeatedly mentioned in one way or another. For example, read Ephesians and note the emphasis in the following verses: 1:9, 10; 2:14-22; 4:4-6, 13. Can you tell what is the main concern of the writer? It is fairly obvious, isn't it? Paul is concerned with unity, and everything he says has to do with unity. Reading the book with this in mind, you will see that it tells how we receive unity, who planned unity, why unity is needed, how God makes unity possible, the result of unity, who should express a life of unity, the attitude needed for a life of unity, the basis of unity, and the spiritual equipment necessary for unity.

As you read each section of Ephesians, you need to ask, "What is Paul saying about unity?" Then you will be understanding the verses or sentences in their proper context. And in that context, you will be able to make an application to your modern-day living.

Now don't think you will immediately and easily be able to decide the theme of each New Testament book. It will take much time and practice. It will require that you share your ideas with others and that they share their ideas with you. It would be very profitable if a whole Sunday school class or Bible-study group would determine the main theme of a Bible book together before considering the passages selected for the lessons.

What's Going On There?

Not only is it important to get a bird's-eye view of a Bible book to understand a passage from it, but it is important also to determine what was going on in the lives of the first readers: that is, to see the historical situation. This could be called getting the "people context" of a passage.

The writers of the Bible wrote with people in mind. They wrote in reference to particular situations or problems. They wanted to help their readers, and they put their thoughts on the scrolls with that in mind.

How can we discover what was going on in the lives of people who lived nearly two thousand years ago? I can hear you saying, "Go to a Bible dictionary or commentary and read what it says about what was going on in Ephesus,

Colossae, or Philippi. Right?" Wrong! That is not the place to begin.

The place to begin is in the writing itself. In each book or letter, you can get an idea about what the situation was by facing each section of Scripture with this question: "What was going on in the lives of the first readers that caused the writer of this letter to say this to them in this way?" This is exactly what you would do with an ordinary letter.

Let me illustrate. Suppose you read a letter from my mother to me that sounded like this:

> I hope Randy is feeling better. I'm sorry he has missed so much school. I'll bet he is really sad to miss such good sledding weather. Do you think Rena and Rhonda will catch it? It's going around here, too. I'll never forget when you got it, Knofel. I thought it was just a rash at first. I'm sending Randy a little gift (a coloring book) to let him know that grandmother is thinking about him. Love, Mother.

From this portion of the letter you can draw several conclusions about the historical situation:

Who is Randy?
Child or adult?
What sex?
What relationship to the writer?
What about his health?
Is the sickness contagious?
What time of the year is it?
Who are Rena and Rhonda?

Undoubtedly you have analyzed the situation correctly. But notice that your conclusions were not directly stated in the letter. You assumed the answers from the statements and questions that were written.

Why aren't those conclusions plainly stated in the letter? Because when my mother wrote to me, she knew that I knew the situation.

If someone would pick up that letter two thousand years from now, he would be able to reconstruct the historical situation just as you did by asking, "Why did she say that in that way?"

Each New Testament writer wrote in the same manner. The author did not have to describe the specific situation he was addressing because the readers already knew it. Now we pick up one of these letters—written first to someone else—and from what is said and the way it is said we can understand fairly accurately the particular situation the first readers were facing.

Before we can ask, "How does this Scripture apply to us?" we must ask, "How did it apply to the first readers in the situation they were facing?" Then we can apply what was said to them in their situation to us who are in a similar situation today.

It is easy to take a verse of Scripture out of its historical context and apply it to a current situation that has no similarity to the situation of the first readers. If a verse was written to help with a problem of disunity, then that is how it ought to be applied today. We should not use a verse for just anything without regard for the purpose for which it was written.

Exercise

Take the biblical letter of Philippians and determine the historical situation of its first readers. Many commentators say the church at Philippi was a trouble-free church, but I think you will discover that it had problems just as the rest of us do.

Read the passages listed on the chart on the next page. Then ask who is being discussed and what is going on in the lives of the first readers.

To help you pull this study together, I will ask and discuss some penetrating questions.

Text	Who Is Being Discussed?	What Is the Situation?
1:12, 13		
1:14-18		
1:27		
2:2-4		
2:5-11		
2:14		
2:25-30		
3:1-3		
3:13-15		
4:2		
4:10-20		

1. Why did Paul feel he had to say the following?

Conduct yourselves in a manner worthy of the gospel of Christ. Then . . . I will know that you stand firm in one spirit, contending as one man for the faith of the gospel (Philippians 1:27).

I suggest that the Philippians were lacking in Christian conduct and were not demonstrating a life of unity. Instead of "contending as one man for the faith," they must have been contending against each other.

2. Why did Paul repeat the emphasis on unity in 2:2? There must have been some disunity.

3. What was going on that would prompt Paul to talk about considering others more important than self, looking out for others' interests, and serving others? (2:3-11). Isn't it clear that selfishness and arrogance were preventing some of the members from serving one another as Christians ought to do?

Some also were complaining and arguing (2:14). There were false teachers among them who were trying to say that a Christian is mature only if he is circumcised properly (3:1-3) and keeps the Jewish traditions (3:4-11). There were some who thought they had reached the height of spiritual maturity, so Paul told them that he himself hadn't (3:12-14). He told them the mark of maturity is the attitude of still "pressing on" (3:14). Evidently, joy was not a dominant feature of the congregation, for Paul kept repeating, "Rejoice, rejoice" (2:18; 3:1; 4:4).

4. Can you determine what events were causing the disunity in the congregation? One, of course, was the false teaching discussed in 3:2. Another one is found by studying three sections that show Paul's concern. Study these three passages and decide on the main topic of each: Philippians 1:12, 13; 2:25-30; 4:10-20.

In 4:10-20, we see that the church at Philippi had sent Paul financial aid, and this was not the first time. Why do you suppose Paul said, "I am not saying this because I am in need, for I have learned to be content whatever the circumstances" (4:11)? Where was Paul? He was in prison (1:12, 13). How do you suppose a congregation would react when asked to send financial aid to an evangelist in prison? Can't you just hear them? "Why don't we send our support to someone who can use it more effectively? How can Paul use it in prison?"

Paul assured them at the beginning of the letter that his imprisonment had advanced the gospel (1:12, 13). Why would he feel the need to do that? Because he wanted them to know that their support was not going to be wasted, even though he was in prison.

In 2:25-30 we see that the Philippians not only had sent money; they also had sent one of the leaders in their congregation, Epaphroditus. I imagine many of the members questioned the wisdom of sending him to help Paul in prison. And then he had to be sent home early. Can't you hear the critics? "We told you it was silly to send him!" So Paul explained carefully why Epaphroditus was coming home early, and he said to the congregation, "Welcome him in the Lord with great joy, and honor men like him" (2:29).

Paul wrote a letter that communicated to the readers what God most wanted them to hear and obey in light of their situation. Paul was concerned about their disunity and about criticism of sending him support and manpower while he was in prison. That's the reason he spent so much time on those topics in such a short letter.

Now with the historical situation in mind, we can apply the book of Philippians to our current living. When some of the members of the church are complaining, criticizing, and disrupting the unity, the admonitions in Philippians need to be applied: consider others more important than yourself, look out for the interests of others, be servants to one another, quit grumbling, and don't think you have arrived at full spiritual maturity.

The book of Philippians came alive before your very eyes, didn't it? This is just a taste of how exciting Bible study can be!

Total Commitment

Isn't Bible study fascinating? And aren't you thrilled with your new understanding? Aren't you excited when you see how you are growing as you apply the meaning you find in the Word?

When you hold the Bible in your hands, you are holding a library of sixty-six of the most important books in the world. But those books are absolutely worthless unless we get our minds into them and they get into our minds.

And yet just getting Bible content into our minds is not enough. We must also allow that content to move through our minds to our behavior. This calls for commitment—commitment that says, "Not my will, but yours be done" (Luke 22:42). But how can we do God's will unless we know what his will is? We can read of his revealed will in the Bible and then determine to live out his will in our lives.

God wills that we be hungry for righteousness (Matthew 5:6). How hungry are you? Are you hungry enough to expend arduous effort in Bible study? Are you hungry enough to work for righteousness? It is God's will that we love him with all our hearts, all our souls, and all our minds (Matthew 22:37). We are to love God not only with our feelings, but also with our intellect. Only then can we have total commitment.

Questions for Discussion

1. Think of a skill you learned at some time in your life. It may be a skill you use on your job, in a hobby, or some other activity. How did you learn it? How much did you improve with practice? How is learning to study the Bible like this skill?

2. In the next week, read the prison epistles (Ephesians, Philippians, Colossians, Philemon) in one sitting each. Write down the main subject of each book. If you are studying this book with a group, compare your answers with those of others in the group. If there are differences, try to determine whether the concepts are similar enough to be slightly different aspects of the same idea. If so, how does sharing the ideas help to clarify the main point? If they are very different, why? Is there a lack of understanding somewhere? What do you do about such differences?

3. Why is it necessary to determine what was going on in the lives of the first readers of the biblical epistles? What are some dangers in interpreting Scripture by what we *assume* was going on?

4. Read the "letter" from the author's mother (page 46). The author points out that several things can be determined about his historical situation from the letter. Are there also some things that *cannot* be determined? For example, which of the following questions can you answer with certainty?
   •Does Randy have measles, chicken pox, or something else?

• Are Randy, Rena, and Rhonda the only children the author has, or are there others who have already had the disease and are now immune?
• Are Rena and Rhonda both daughters of the author, or could one of them be his wife?
• What month of the year is it?
How does the uncertainty over these issues caution us about *assumptions* we make in Bible study?

5. Complete the chart on page 48. How does this analysis help you appreciate the message of Philippians? Make a similar chart for Colossians.

6. The author suggests Paul told the Philippians to conduct themselves "in a manner worthy of the gospel" and that they "stand firm . . . contending as one man for the faith" (1:27) because they were not doing so. What are some other possible explanations? (For example, does a football coach shout to his team, "Now go out there and win!" because the players do not know that is what they are supposed to do?) How do you decide which option is most likely when more than one explanation is possible.

7. Do you have the "total commitment" required to make Bible study Bible application? What do you need to do to deepen that commitment? How can a study group help you?

Step Four

Putting Things Into Place

By now you may be thinking, "Whew! If I do all that this book suggests, I will have to read through each Bible book a dozen times!" Yes, at first you will have to read and reread; but once you become comfortable with the study system, reading a book once or twice will suffice because you will know what to look for.

Looking for the theme of a book and discovering the historical situation of the first readers will come naturally for you as you continue to discipline yourself in this type of study. Soon all the pieces will fall into place. It will become as natural to you as reading a letter from a friend.

What we read in the letters of Paul and others was written to people just like us. What was written in the four Gospels tells people just like us what Jesus said and did to and for people just like us.

Women did not attend school in Jesus' day. But even without schooling they appreciated Jesus' teaching (Luke 8:1-3).

Fishermen, soldiers, government employees, house-wives, young children, lepers, and the poor—all loved to hear him. Multitudes came from many miles to listen to his teaching. It would be easy to think that great throngs of people came to see his spectacular miracles, and of course some of them did. But notice how often hearing is put before healing.

> The people [were] crowding around him and listening. . . . crowds of people came to hear him and to be healed. . . . A large crowd of his disciples . . . and a great number of people . . . who had come to hear him and to be healed . . . (Luke 5:1, 15; 6:17, 18).

They came, thousands of them, to hear Jesus. And what they heard, we can read in the Gospels. If those people could understand what Jesus said, we can. Of course, they *wanted* to listen. They walked many miles, camped out, and went without food to hear him. On one occasion they stayed with Jesus three days. Even after they ran out of food, they stayed (Matthew 15:32). They had to hear him!

That situation seems rare today. If the sermon on Sunday goes ten minutes longer than usual, we get upset with the preacher. If we are encouraged to read the Bible half an hour a day, we don't see how we can work it in. If we are going to know God's Word and his will, we must *want* to listen to him. Wouldn't it be wonderful to enter Heaven fully accustomed to listening to and understanding God's Word?

Hanging Together

After we determine the main theme of a book and the specific situation the first readers were facing, we can more clearly understand what was written if we study how the writer has put his book or letter together. How does the written material move along? How do the thoughts fit together?

A primary way to discover how a book hangs together is to notice all the connecting words. After much study, I am tempted to say that the connecting words are probably the most important words in the text. Perhaps that would be an overstatement, but connecting words deserve more attention than they usually get. The connecting word tells us immediately how the following sentence or phrase fits into the picture. The connectors tie the thoughts together in just the way God wants them tied together.

Many doctrinal questions could be solved if we would pay more attention to the connecting words in a passage. For instance, we never read in the Gospels that Jesus healed *by* (by means of) casting out demons. Instead we read that he healed *and* (also) cast out demons. The connecting word *and* tells us that Jesus performed two separate, distinct actions. When we take note of that, we see that it is a mistake to suppose, as some students do, that the people of Jesus' time thought illnesses were caused by demons and healed by getting rid of demons.

One of the major fallacies of modern translations is that they delete many of these important connecting words. God inspired the connecting words so we would not have to guess how the thoughts were tied together. Therefore (a connecting word), it is important to compare several versions.

On the chart on page 56 are several of the important connecting words and their meanings. It would be advisable for you to jot these down on a piece of paper and tape the list inside your Bible, or secure it with a paper clip, so you can refer to it often.

When you see one of these connecting words, you know that to understand the sentence or phrase in which it appears, you must notice the preceding sentence or phrase, because it is related in some way. The connecting word shows how it is related.

Here is an example: "*For* all of you who were baptized into Christ have clothed yourselves with Christ" (Galatians 3:27, NASB). The connecting word *for* indicates a reason for something. The reason for what? Read the preceding verse:

Word	Function
For Because Since	Reason or explanation. *Example: It is dark **because** it is night.*
Until	Limitation. *Example: It is dark **until** dawn.*
Then So then Therefore Wherefore	Result. *Example: The sun has gone down, **therefore** it is getting dark.*
So that That In order that For	Purpose. *Example: The sun was created **in order that** we may have light.*
But Much more Nevertheless However	Contrast. *Example: It is dark, **but** not so dark as last night.*
Although	Concession. *Example: **Although** it is dark, I will go out.*
By Through	Means of something. *Example: **By** the light we can see the world.*
Accordingly Likewise As Even as	Comparison. *Example: Black is **just as** dark **as** night.*
And Also	Addition. *Example: They are seen at night **and** during the day.*

"For you are all sons of God through faith in Christ Jesus."
Being baptized into Christ and thus clothed with Christ is
the reason we are sons of God. No one has the right to read
verse 26 and conclude that baptism is not a part of becoming a child of God. In that verse, the connecting word
through shows us that faith is the *means* by which we become children of God, but baptism is *when* it happens.

Notice that verse 26 also begins with *for*. This verse is
explaining what is said in verse 25, so we must read that

verse to get the complete meaning. "But now that faith has come, we are no longer under a tutor." Paul can say that in verse 25 because (for) "you are all sons of God" (verse 26).

See how each sentence is built upon another? The connecting words are building blocks. Look back to verse 23 and notice how the connecting words make the whole section hang together. *But* introduces a contrast, *therefore* introduces a result, *that* introduces a purpose, *for* introduces a reason, *through* introduces a means. Look at each one carefully and see what the contrast is, what the result is, what the purpose is, what the reason is, and what the means is.

It is easy to overlook these little words, so I suggest you purchase a cheap paperback edition of the New Testament (or use one of the extra Bibles you have lying around) and circle each connecting word you find as you read. After you complete each paragraph, go back and analyze how the connecting words help the thoughts fit together.

Consequently you are no longer foreigners and aliens, but fellow citizens with God's people and members of God's household . . . (Ephesians 2:19).

Consequently shows results: we are not foreigners and aliens, but are fellow citizens. *But* shows the contrast between our present and former conditions. What produced this result? We must read the preceding sentence:

He came and preached peace to you who were far away and peace to those who were near. For through him we both have access to the Father by one Spirit (Ephesians 2:17, 18).

So we see that *not* being foreigners and *being* fellow-citizens (members of God's household) are the results of having access to the Father by one Spirit.

We can conclude, therefore, that anyone who is united to the Father by the Spirit is a member of God's household. That means we are related to each other spiritually; we are to treat each other as brothers, not as enemies.

Now consider this statement: "Christians are still under the Ten Commandments." Is that true or false? We can determine the answer by noticing the connecting words in the following passage of Scripture:

Why the Law (then?) It was added (because of) transgressions, having been ordained (through) angels (by) the agency (of) a mediator, (until) the seed should come (to) whom the promise had been made (Galatians 3:19, NASB).

The word *until* tells us that the law had a limitation. It was ordained and added "until the seed should come." What is that seed? Look at verse 16. The seed is Jesus. Jesus fulfilled the law so we could be saved by faith.

Now read Galatians 3:23-26, noticing the connecting words and analyzing how the thoughts are tied together. Make your conclusions and answer the above true/false question according to what the Scripture says.

An Exercise

Enlarge the chart on page 58 on an eight-and-a half-by-eleven-inch piece of paper. (Make it twice the size here.) Then read Ephesians 2:13-19 and identify the function of each connecting word and an explanation of what it means in its sentence. (The chart is based on the New American Standard Bible. If you use a different version, you may find some variation in the words, but probably that will make no difference in the function or the explanation.)

To see what I mean, consider this sentence: It is dark until the break of dawn. The connecting word *until* is put on the first line of the chart with its function and an explanation of how it ties together the ideas of the sentence. You can determine the function of each of the other words and briefly explain how they tie together the ideas that go with them in the text of Ephesians. Understanding the relationships

Verse	Word	Function	Explanation
	until	limitation	Shows that darkness ends at dawn
13	but		
13	by		
14	for		
14	and		
15	by		
15	that		
16	and		
16	through		
16	by		
17	and		
17	and		
18	for		
18	through		
19	so that		
19	but		
19	and		

shown by these connecting words, will help you see Paul's message more clearly than you have seen it before.

Organization of Thoughts

Not only must we notice the connecting words in Scripture, but we also must determine how the writer relates his every thought to the main theme of the book. Thus we can understand how it all hangs together.

In Step 3, we discovered that the theme of the book of Ephesians is unity. Now we need to determine how Paul developed this topic, how he organized his thoughts around the main purpose of his writing. We need to find the what, who, how, where, when, and why of the theme of unity in Ephesians. Then it will be natural and relatively easy to outline the book.

The chart below divides the book of Ephesians into major sections for you. Read the sections and write down in the following form what you think each section is saying about unity. To make room for the writing, enlarge the form on a larger sheet of paper.

Scripture	What does it say about unity?
1 :3-8	
1:9, 10	
1:11-14	
1:15-23	
2:1-3	
2:4-10	
2:11-18	
2:19-22	
3:1-13	
3:14-21	
4:1-3	
4:4-6	
4:7-16	
4:17-24	
4:25—5:2	
5:3-21	
5:22—6:4	
6:5-9	
6:10-20	

Now you should be able to outline the book of Ephesians. It might look something like the outline on page 61. You fill in the Scripture text that goes with each point and add the sub-headings.

A lot of work, you say? Yes, but the results are worth it. I am guessing that you know a great deal more than you ever did before about the book of Ephesians. I imagine you have

Outline	Text
I. He who unites us and his blessings	
II. He who planned unity	
III. The need for unity	
IV. The motives of God	
V. What Jesus did to bring unity	
VI. The results of unity	
VII. The apostle of unity	
VIII. Attitudes needed for unity	
IX. Basis of unity	
X. The gifts and unity	
XI. Conduct needed for unity	
XII. Home and unity	
XIII. Work and unity	
XIV. The warfare against unity	

a much better insight on the topic of unity. Perhaps you could now teach a lesson on unity without even consulting a commentary once! And I am assuming that you now can share the meaning of Ephesians with someone else.

A Challenge

Circle your answer to each of the following questions, giving a little thought to each one.

1. Do you believe the Bible is the inspired, infallible Word of God, the only authoritative rule of faith and practice for the Christian?
   Yes   No

2. Is it possible to understand the Bible?
   Yes   No

3. How important is it to understand the Bible?
   a. Very important   c. Like any book
   b. Important   d. Not important

4. How many hours per week do you spend studying the Bible, not counting Sunday school and worship?
   14   10   7   5   3   1   0

5. How many hours per week do you spend reading newspapers, magazines, and books?
   14   10   7   5   3   1   0

6. How many hours per week do you spend watching TV?
   14   10   7   5   3   1   0

7. If you were taught to understand the Bible better, would you spend more time studying it?
   Yes   Probably   No

A Christian brother, Tom Browdy, gave this survey with some other questions to a congregation in Illinois. Two hundred thirty-two people responded, though some did not answer all the questions. All but three respondents were Christians.

Only three of those who answered question one did not think the Bible was inspired. If you answered yes to that question, may I conclude that you give the Bible top priority in your reading?

Out of 226 who answered question two, 220 said it was possible to understand the Bible. One hundred eighty-six out of 227 said it was very important to understand the Bible. Thus far, the Bible was thought of very highly.

Out of 212 people who answered question four, 2 studied the Bible 14 hours a week, 4 studied it 10 hours, 11 studied it 7 hours, 17 studied it 5 hours, 38 studied it 3 hours, and 63 studied it 1 hour. Seventy-seven people said they did not study the Bible at all!

There seems to be a credibility gap when we can say on the one hand that the Bible is God's inspired Word, that it is very important to understand, and that it is possible to understand; but on the other hand we don't spend much time reading it—or maybe none at all! What is even worse, 124 people out of 212 did not answer yes when asked whether they would spend more time reading the Bible if they were taught how to understand it better! I think some priorities need to be straightened out!

Paul told Timothy that if he wanted to be an approved workman in God's business, he had better take care to handle the word of truth correctly (2 Timothy 2:15).

James did say, "Not many of you should . . . be teachers" (James 3:1), but he did not say that not many should become students. Jesus called us to become his disciples. We can't be disciples without being learners. Jesus said, "Take my yoke upon you and *learn* from me" (Matthew 11:29).

We learn from Jesus as we study what he did and what he said and what he inspired others to say. That is the reason we need to spend time learning how to understand the Bible.

At one time, many of Jesus' followers left him. They would not take the time and effort needed to learn from him. As the crowd was leaving, Jesus turned to the Twelve and asked, "You do not want to go away also, do you?"

Peter answered, "Lord, to whom shall we go? You have words of eternal life" (John 6:67, 68).

May that be our answer to Jesus! Let us not sidestep Bible study. Where else can we find the words of eternal life? Given enough time, the death rate for all of us is one hundred percent. To be ready for what is sure to come, we must give top priority to God's Word.

Questions for Discussion

1. The author notes that a wide variety of people loved to hear Jesus: "fishermen, soldiers, government employees, housewives, young children, lepers, and the poor." Do you think the Bible has the same broad appeal that Jesus had? Why or why not? What can you and/or your church do to make Bible study more appealing?

2. How important do you think desire is in understanding the Bible? Why do you think more Christians do not seem to *want* to hear God's Word?

3. Read Ephesians 6 from several translations (at least five). How do the connecting words compare? How does noticing the different ways the connecting words are translated help you understand the passage?

4. Complete the chart on page 59. What new insights on the passage (Ephesians 2:13-19) did noticing the connecting words provide?

5. Complete the chart on page 60. What new insights about unity did you discover? Suggest three or four ways to put into practice the principles found in the book of Ephesians.

6. Read the book of Philippians and outline it in the same way the author did the book of Ephesians.
   •Make a chart like the one for Ephesians on page 60. Instead of "Unity," write what Philippians says about "Joy."
   •Make an outline like the one on page 61.

7. Complete the survey on page 62. What does it reveal about your priorities? What can you do to improve?

8. Read 2 Timothy 2:15. What kind of "workman" are you? How well do you handle God's Word? What will you do this week to improve?

Step Five

Studying Topics and Words

Hurry, hurry! Run, run, run! Our world is busy and complex. There is much to do and little time in which to do it. Finding time to read and study the Bible is difficult.

But wait a minute! Remember the last two questions of the survey in the last chapter? How much time per week do you spend reading newspapers, magazines, and books? How much time do you spend watching television? In the congregation surveyed, 127 out of 217 spent 7 hours or more a week watching television, while only 17 spent that much time on Bible study. While 52 people spent at least 14 hours watching television, only 2 people studied the Bible that much. Only 6 Christians did not read newspapers, magazines, and books. Only 5 did not watch television. But 72 Christians did not read the Bible!

By considering the figures, you might think most Christians believe television is inspired by God and is the only rule of faith and practice. Obviously, time is not really our problem. We have the Bible, we have the tools, and we have the time. We *can* understand the Bible, but we *must* study it.

━━━━━━━━━━━━━━━━━━━━━

How to Study Biblical Topics

One reason some people have difficulty understanding the Bible is that it uses words and concepts that are not common in our secular society. It introduces to us many topics that are not discussed elsewhere, but we can understand them. Have you ever wished you could find out everything the Bible says about sin, Heaven, Hell, love, baptism, marriage, divorce, death, God, church, speaking in tongues, healing, or demons? How big do you think your library would have to be to cover these subjects? Just two books are all you need—the Bible and an exhaustive concordance.

An exhaustive concordance lists most of the words in the Bible. It lists the words alphabetically, and lists every place the words are used in the Bible. By using this tool, you can find everything the Bible says about a topic.

Make or purchase three by five note cards for keeping a record of your research. On the upper right-hand corner of a card, write a Scripture reference (which you found in the concordance) in which God speaks about the topic. In the upper left-hand corner, write the topic and subtopic you are researching. On the main portion of the card, write the basic idea of what that particular Scripture passage says about the topic. One caution—be sure to read the verse in context (read several sentences before and after the verse, and determine the theme and historical situation of the Bible book). Otherwise you may misunderstand the verse.

For example, let us say you want to research the topic of baptism. The concordance cites Acts 2:38 as one of the verses that mention baptism: "Peter replied, 'Repent and be baptized, every one of you, in the name of Jesus Christ for the forgiveness of your sins. And you will receive the gift of the Holy Spirit.'" You note on your cards several ideas (these are subtopics): Who was speaking? What is to precede baptism? In whose name are we baptized? What is the result of baptism? It is best to use one note card for each subtopic—like this:

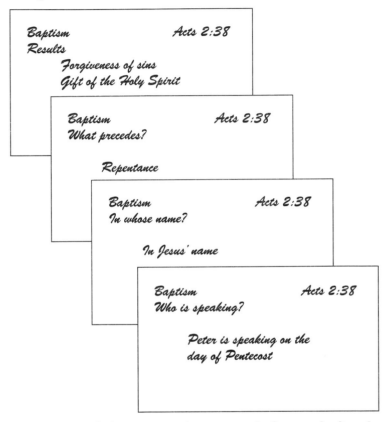

As you read the context (sentences before and after the verse), you discover that Peter told the people to repent and be baptized after they believed in Jesus as Christ and Lord (Acts 2:36, 37). The people were baptized after Peter told them to be saved (Acts 2:40, 41). So what can you conclude? Is baptism related to one's salvation?

After you research the topic of baptism, taking notes in this manner for every verse in which baptism is mentioned, then you can organize your note cards by placing together all those that record information under the same topics, like what precedes baptism, results of baptism, and others. Then, using the cards, you can write in an organized manner your conclusions about baptism and what you have learned about the topic—all based on what the Bible says, not what some teacher has told you in the past.

Following these steps, you will be well on your way toward in-depth Bible study. Why not select one topic a week to research in this way?

Shortcuts

Several publishers have made available computer software that does the work of a concordance electronically. You may also speed up the process of studying biblical topics with a topical Bible or a study Bible. A topical Bible lists Scripture passages by topics, similar to the way a concordance lists passages by words. You can use a topical Bible with a variety of translations because it does not depend on precise word agreement. It will, however, be slanted to the editors' own understanding of the Scripture passages. You may or may not agree that a passage addresses the topic under which it is listed in a topical Bible. *Nave's Topical Bible* has long been regarded as the classic work in this field. It is available from a variety of publishers.

Study Bibles are designed to give a variety of study help within an edition of the Bible. The *Thompson Chain Reference Bible* and the *Open Bible* are popular study Bibles available in several versions. The *NIV Study Bible* also is a very helpful work.

Biblical Word Study

In addition to studying biblical topics, we must study the meaning of biblical words. It is one thing to know everything the Bible says about baptism, but it is something else to know what the word *baptism* itself means.

The best way to discover the meaning of a word is to study how it is used. Can you tell from the way *baptism* is used in Scripture what it meant to the first-century readers?

Vine's *Expository Dictionary of New Testament Words* is an excellent, helpful tool for this type of study. The words appear alphabetically. The Greek words from which an English word is translated are given; then the meaning is discussed with some texts. For instance, Vine devotes more than a page to baptism. His first sentence includes this: "Baptism, consisting of the processes of immersion, submersion, and emergence (from *bapto*, to dip)" (page 96).

Other fine tools for word study include William Barclay's set of commentaries and his *More New Testament Words*, Ralph Earle's *Word Meanings in the New Testament* (arranged by text), and Colin Brown's three-volume *Dictionary of New Testament Theology* (arranged alphabetically). For some deeper study, Tyndale's *Word Study Concordance* and its companion *Word Study New Testament* are very helpful. The *Index to Brown, Driver and Briggs' Hebrew Lexicon* allows the non-Hebrew student to use the classic Hebrew lexicon for Old Testament word studies.

The following paragraphs are a sampling of how the study of biblical words can make the Bible come alive for you.

1. *Meek.* "Blessed are the meek" (Matthew 5:5, King James Version). I used to think a meek person was a weak person. But in the first century the word was used in describing the training of wild horses. A wild horse would buck any time he wanted to; he was impulsive. When he was "broken," he was called a meek horse. This meant he now had his temperament under control. He was as strong as ever, but he wasn't impulsive and out of control. He would not have selfish temper tantrums. His power was controlled by the reins of his master.

2. *Mystery.* In English we use this word to mean something that is unknown, and often a detective is trying to find the unknown. But the biblical word means something that is known, not by detective work, but because it has been revealed (disclosed). *Mystery* was the word used to

describe the many pieces of a plan that had been put together so the whole plan could be seen. A good translation of the word would be "strategy." So when we read that God has "made known to us the mystery of his will" (Ephesians 1:9), we know it means that God has put together all the pieces of his plan from the book of Genesis on—and we can see how those pieces fit together.

3. *Pledge* or *Guarantee.* "Who is given as a pledge of our inheritance" (Ephesians 1:14, NASB). The word *pledge* in the New American Standard Bible is translated *earnest* in the King James Version, *guarantee* in the Revised Standard, and *deposit guaranteeing* in the New International. All these English words are very similar in meaning.

The Greek word was used in the first century to describe the down payment or earnest money for a purchase. That payment guaranteed that other payments would follow until the bill was paid in full. We do the same today. When we promise to buy a house, we put down earnest money or a deposit. That money guarantees that we will carry out our pledge to purchase the house.The house is taken off the market, and the Realtor will not sell it to another person.

Using the Concordance

To determine the meaning of a word, we should also use another tool—an exhaustive concordance. To find out what a biblical word meant to the first readers, we must find the meaning of that word in its original language (Greek for the New Testament, Hebrew for the Old Testament). With a concordance (Young's or Strong's), you can do this even if you do not know one word of Greek or Hebrew.

In the following paragraphs I will illustrate how to use Young's concordance (Strong's is a bit different). We will start with the English word *gifts* in 1 Corinthians 12:4: "Now there are diversities of *gifts,* but the same Spirit" (KJV).

1. Look up the word *gift* in the concordance (page 390). You will see that the English word is used to represent several different Hebrew and Greek words. At the moment you are not interested in all of them, but only the one used in 1 Corinthians 12:4. So go on with step 2.

2. Find 1 Corinthians 12:4 in the listing under *gift* (near the top of the third column, page 390). You will notice it is listed under heading #21, "Grace, favor, kindness." Those three words show three different ways to translate the same Greek word. In other words, *gift* in 1 Corinthians 12:4 could have been *grace, favor,* or *kindness.* Now you can begin to see the basic meaning of that particular word.

3. Jot down all the other Scripture references under heading #21. But before looking them up in the Bible, you want to know where the same Greek word is used with a different translation. So go on with step 4.

4. Look again at that heading. On the same line you can see the Greek word, and following it you can see how it would be spelled in English letters: *charisma.* You don't need to pronounce it, but if you want to, say "Car-ISS-mah."

5. At the back of the concordance are alphabetical listings of all the Hebrew and Greek words in their English spelling. These sections are entitled "Index-Lexicon to the Old Testament" and Index-Lexicon to the New Testament," which begins on page 57. Find *charisma* (bottom of fourth column, page 63) There you will find every way that word is translated into English in the King James Version. It is translated *free gift* twice and *gift* fifteen times.

6. You have already found the fifteen references for *gift* (step 3 above). Go back to the main part of the concordance and find *free gift* (second column, page 373). Jot down the two Scripture references there. Now you have found every place where God inspired the word *charisma* to be used in the New Testament.

7. Use your note cards and research what every Scripture reference says about *charisma-gift.* From your study, answer these questions: What are the *charisma*-type gifts? Who has them? Why? How are the gifts given? Do you have them?

With the concordance, you can know the Hebrew or Greek word from which every English word came. Without one day of Hebrew or Greek class, you can research every topic or word in the Bible. What is needed is your interest, time, and commitment.

Questions for Discussion

1. What are some ways you can make more time for Bible study? What leisure activities can you cut out?
2. Look up the word *repentance* (including alternate forms like *repent, repents, repenting*) in an exhaustive concordance. Look up each reference and make a set of note cards like the ones described on page 67 to make a file on the word. What is repentance? How is it related to salvation? When is it appropriate for the Christian?
3. Look up *miracle* in *Young's Analytical Concordance.* How many headings (Hebrew/Greek words) are listed for this one word? What do the different terms tell you about the nature of miracles? Why do you think the word for "sign" has more citations than the heading for "acts of power"?
4. The fifth heading for *miracle* is "sign" (Greek, *semeion*). Look up a number of references where the same word is translated differently (not "miracle"). For example, the word is used for Paul's autograph (KJV, "token") in 2 Thessalonians 3:17. What do you think this suggests about the purpose of miracles?
5. The author says, "Without one day of Hebrew or Greek class, you can research every topic or word in the Bible." What value is there to studying Greek and/or Hebrew?
6. The author further notes that "what is needed is your interest, time, and commitment." How willing are you to invest interest, time, and commitment? What can you do this week to demonstrate such a commitment?

Step Six

Considering the Customs

Paul once wrote to Timothy about some people who had a "form of godliness" and were influential enough to enter into people's homes and teach, but who were "always learning and never able to come to a knowledge of the truth" (2 Timothy 3:5-8, NASB). Because of their attitude of selfishness, arrogance, and boastfulness, they would never know the truth (2 Timothy 3:2).

It is very difficult for such a person to change any of his ideas. He says, "Don't bother me with facts; my mind is made up. I know I'm right; if your conclusions don't square with mine, you are wrong." Such people often "oppose the truth"; and as long as they continue in this way, "they will not make further progress" (2 Timothy 3:8, 9, NASB).

To know the truth, we need a learning attitude. We must be willing to admit we are wrong sometimes. We must be committed to God's truth, not to our own opinions. We must take advantage of every opportunity to learn.

Jesus told his disciples (learners) they needed to become like little children. Children know they don't know everything, and so they are teachable. We too must become like children if we want to come to a knowledge of the truth.

Customs of Bible Times

In our search for the truth of God's Word, thus far we have dealt with aspects inherent in the written Word itself. In this chapter, we will consider some of the customs of Bible times and try to see how this knowledge of them will illuminate the Word for us.

The Bible was written thousands of years ago to people who lived in a time and culture different from ours. They did not have instant foods, automatic appliances, huge supermarkets, automobiles, polyester knits, or jet planes. The writing in the Bible relates to their customs and culture, not ours. Still it relates to the attitudes and actions of people today no less than it did to those of the people then.

In making application of what the Bible says to us in our time and culture, it helps a great deal to understand the customs of the people who lived at the time the Bible was written. I do not mean we must transfer the practice of those customs to all nations for all times, but I feel we can transfer to our own culture an application of the principles taught amidst the customs and culture of Bible times.

It is not very difficult to find information about ancient customs. There are many good books on the subject (see Step 1). To whet your appetite, I will discuss briefly some of the customs. Try to make application to your life today.

Money in New Testament Times

Did you ever wonder why the disciples did not want to spend two hundred pennies to feed the crowd? (John 6:7, King James Version). Two dollars doesn't sound like much to feed thousands of people, does it? A footnote in some versions says, "A *denarius* was worth about twenty cents." That still doesn't seem like much, but it is completely misleading to compare a penny or a *denarius* with today's money in Great Britain or in the United States.

A penny, or *denarius,* was the amount a laborer in Jesus' time earned in one day. When the disciples said two hundred pennies, they were talking about two hundred days' pay. To realize why they balked, multiply the average day's pay in your area by two hundred. Then suggest that the church spend that much money on one barbecue for the community, and you will get the same reaction that Jesus got from his disciples!

Now read Acts 19:19. A Greek *drachma* was worth about as much as a Roman *denarius*—a day's pay. So multiply a modern day's pay by fifty thousand to see the value of the books that were burned. Why do you suppose the Ephesians burned them? Why didn't they just sell them?

Do we have books that ought to be burned because of the bad influence they may have? The Ephesian magicians not only burned their books; they gave up their business, their way of making a living. Do any of us have jobs or businesses that ought to be sacrificed? Can anyone have a strong Christian influence when he runs a bar, a tobacco shop, or an adult bookstore? Think of the money a person would lose if he gave up such a business. Then think of the Ephesian magicians. Does our commitment measure up to theirs?

The Second Mile

Jesus talked about going a second mile (Matthew 5:41). What does that mean? In Jesus' day, Palestine was under Roman occupation. The Roman law allowed a Roman soldier to enlist any Jew to carry the soldier's gear for one mile. The Jews hated the Romans. It was degrading to have to carry a Roman soldier's things. In fact, a Jew who had to do so was made religiously unclean and had to undergo a special ceremony of cleansing afterwards.

Naturally, the Jews avoided this duty like the plague! When they did get "caught," don't you suppose they knew exactly how many steps made up one mile? They counted each and every step and would not go one step farther than a mile. But Jesus said, "Go a second mile." In other words, go beyond what is required of you.

Can you make the application to us today? What if you detest making coffee for the boss every day? Jesus might say, "Make the coffee and take it to the boss's desk and smile!"

Washing Feet

In Jesus' day people traveled by walking or by riding on animals or in chariots. Regardless of the mode of transportation, they would arrive at their destination with tired and dusty feet. Therefore the host at the destination would provide water and a towel so the traveler could refresh his feet. Sometimes a servant was assigned to wash the guest's feet. It was an act of kindness. It said, "You are welcome. Make yourself comfortable."

If you have ever walked all day at the state fair, or been shopping all day, or been on a big hunting trip through swamps and up mountains, you know how their feet must have felt and how refreshing it was to wash and dry them.

Very seldom did one person wash another person's feet, unless he was a slave commanded to do the lowly task. But Jesus washed the disciples' feet and said they should follow his example (John 13:1-15). The Lord was willing to humble himself to the lowest position for the good of his followers. His own status was not the issue.

Guidelines for Application

As we consider the customs of Bible times, we need to know when to carry over into our time and culture the exact practice and when to carry over the principle that is expressed. In the case of John 13, which "example" did Jesus mean that we should follow—the literal washing of feet or the general principle of serving others? This is difficult to determine and has been a source of discussion, dispute, and division among Christians for centuries. Let me suggest the following guidelines:

1. Is the custom different elsewhere in the Bible? If so, it is cultural and temporary. For instance, in the Old Testament a woman wearing a veil was a prostitute (Genesis 38:14, 15); but in the New Testament a married woman would wear a veil and a loose woman would not (1 Corinthians 11:1-7). We may conclude that the custom of wearing a veil is cultural and temporary.

2. Is the custom or command connected with becoming a Christian, as is repentance or baptism? If so, it is for all cultures and all times, though it makes no difference whether the baptizing is done in a river or lake, a baptistery or ocean.

3. Read the entire context of a Scripture passage to find out whether the Scripture itself gives any clue as to whether a practice or custom is or is not cultural and temporary. For example, Paul's writing in 1 Corinthians 7:25-35 is clearly his advice for people to remain single in their present distressing situation (verse 26). Paul certainly does not mean people should never marry.

4. Could another action in a different culture fulfill the same purpose and principle that the custom fulfilled in Bible times? For example, greeting one another with a hug or handshake in our culture may be the same as greeting one another with a kiss in the New Testament culture (Romans 16:16).

5. Was the custom varied in Bible times and still approved? Praying with lifted hands is mentioned in 1 Timothy 2:8, but that was not the only acceptable posture for prayer. In Gethsemane Jesus knelt and fell on his face (Luke 22:41; Matthew 26:39). But the Bible gives no hint of more than one mode of baptism.

6. Notice the emphasis placed upon the custom by the apostles. If they mentioned it only incidentally, we can

hardly consider it essential. Perhaps the principle of it can be applied as well or better in a different action.

7. Study all the biblical references to the custom. If there is variety in the practice of the custom, you can be pretty sure that the custom is cultural and temporary. As an illustration, Paul spoke about women keeping silent, but in other Scriptural passages we read that God used women as leaders and prophets.

So what of washing feet? Use the criteria above to state how this passage of Scripture should be applied.

Conclusion

Jesus' teachings were delivered to us through the first-century culture—with leaven, lamps, lambs, yokes, and other items of antiquity—but the principles of his teachings apply to his followers in every century, even people who will never see a lamb or light a lamp. Knowing the culture of Bible times makes the Bible come alive with application and meaning for us.

The Bible will change your culture if you commit your customs to God as the people of old did. Let your culture be a Christ-centered culture, even amidst the commuter trains and cellular telephones. He is big enough to be Lord of all!

Questions for Discussion

1. In introducing the subject of considering the customs of the biblical era, the author reminds us of Jesus' command to become like children. How is the metaphor of children appropriate for many of us when we think about the customs of antiquity?

2. Make a list of "second mile" activities that you have done—situations where you went beyond what was expected to meet the needs of another. Was it pleasant or tedious? Why? For whom are you most likely to go the second mile? Why?
3. Review the author's suggestions for applying customs/principles from Bible times to our own culture. (They are listed below.) Would you add or subtract anything? Why or why not?

1. Is the custom different elsewhere in the Bible?

2. Is the custom or command connected with becoming a Christian?

3. Read the entire context of a Scripture passage to find out whether the Scripture itself gives any clue as to whether a practice or custom is or is not cultural and temporary.

4. Could another action in a different culture fulfill the same purpose and principle that the custom fulfilled in Bible times?

5. Was the custom varied in Bible times and still approved?

6. Notice the emphasis placed upon the custom by the apostles.

7. Study all the biblical references to the custom.

4. Use the criteria above (with any revisions you may have made) to answer the question the author raised about John 13. Should we apply the practice—washing feet—or the principle—lowly service? Suggest some tangible ways to implement the application.
5. The author says, "The Bible will change your culture if you commit your customs to God. . . ." What customs can you and your church "commit to God" to begin to make some changes in our culture? How can you do that?

Step Seven

Considering the Style

What we think and who we are (our characters) are more closely related than most people realize. Our characters are formed from whatever our minds habitually take in. That is the reason Paul wrote, "Set your minds on the things above, not on earthly things" (Colossians 3:2). It's the reason he said:

> Finally, brothers, whatever is true, whatever is noble, whatever is right, whatever is pure, whatever is lovely, whatever is admirable—if anything is excellent or praiseworthy, think about such things (Philippians 4:8).

It follows, then, that the more we read God's Word, the more we will become as he is. The psalmist expressed the thought in this way: "Thy word I have treasured in my heart [mind], that I may not sin against Thee" (Psalm 119:11, NASB). Simply deciding that God's Word hss value will not cause us to live righteously. No, to treasure God's Word in our minds means to deposit it there just as we would deposit money in a bank.

Depositing the treasure in our minds takes effort. Too often we leave Bible study until just before bedtime, when our minds are tired and not functioning at full capacity. This is not the way to secure the treasure of God's Word in our minds. For the treasure to be firmly deposited, we must be teachable, learning from others and sharing what we learn. We must not only read, but also meditate upon the Word (Psalm 119:15), and the treasure of God's Word will be pure delight to us (Psalm 119:16). The treasure will become part of our behavior and character as we obey and remember what we read and study.

Let us determine that with our minds we will seek, learn, meditate, delight in God's Word, obey it, and remember it. Are we more willing to commit ourselves to twenty-five years of systematically paying for our houses than to twenty-five years of a systematic study of God's Word? Consider which activity will have eternal value.

Writing Styles of the Bible

The Bible is not simply a single book written by one author with one style. It is a collection of books by many authors with varied styles. In order to understand the language of the Bible fully, we must consider the ways (styles) in which it was written.

Picturesque Speech

Nearly all writers and speakers use picturesque speech (figures of speech) that they do not intend for their readers or listeners to take literally. They mean for the readers and listeners to understand that the language is symbolic. For people familiar with the symbolism, the figures are an aid to understanding. The pictures they create in the mind are expressive and meaningful even though they are not literal.

Imagine what would happen if we took the following figures of speech literally: the sun is setting; it's raining cats and dogs; that argument doesn't hold water; I'm tickled to death; you're a scream; you're sharp as a tack; you lie like a rug; white as a sheet; hot as a firecracker; cold as an iceberg; his mind is a steel trap; quick as lightning; you're pulling my leg.

In the literature of the Bible we can find figures of speech that also are to be taken symbolically, not literally. Of course, this problem arises: how do we know when to take the Bible literally and when to consider the language symbolic? Here are some guidelines:

1. Is the literal interpretation absurd? Jesus said, "I am the door" (John 10:7, KJV). It would be ridiculous to think of Jesus as a block of wood with hinges and a knob, so this must be figurative.

2. Would a literal interpretation contradict other teachings? Jesus advised cutting off a hand (Matthew 5:30). Taken literally, that would violate other teachings about caring for our bodies and resisting temptation (1 Corinthians 6:18-20; 10:13). Again, this is figurative.

3. Does the immediate context (verses surrounding) tell us what the interpretation should be? When Jesus spoke about destroying the temple, the text tells us he was referring to his body (John 2:18-21). Once again, the expression is figurative.

4. Does the Bible interpret the symbol elsewhere? Many of the symbols in the book of Revelation are explained in the book itself. The seven golden lampstands (Revelation 1:12) are churches (1:20). The woman (17:3) is a city (17:5). The waters (17:1) are peoples (17:15).

5. Interpret God's Word literally unless you have a clear reason to take it symbolically. The most important thing to ask is this: what point is this picturesque speech trying to communicate to us?

Following are examples of figures of speech that are found in the Bible. See if you can decide what truth God is communicating in each.

Two Things Are Compared

    a. God is called a "rock" (Psalm 42:9)
    b. A man will be "like a tree planted by streams of water" (Psalm 1:3).
    c. "The earthly tent we live in" (2 Corinthians 5:1).
    d. "His chest is hard as rock" (Job 41:24).
    e. "Stiff-necked" (Acts 7:51).
    f. Faith "as a mustard seed" (Matthew 17:20).
    g. "He will be like the dew to Israel" (Hosea 14:5).
    h. "I am a worm" (Psalm 22:6).
    i. The devil is "like a roaring lion" (1 Peter 5:8).

A Thing Is Given Personal Characteristics

    a. "Let the distant shores rejoice" (Psalm 97:1).
    b. "Let the mountains sing together for joy" (Psalm 98:8).

Part of a Person's Body Is Used for the Whole Person

    a. "You will bring my gray head down to the grave in sorrow" (Genesis 42:38).
    b. "The government will be on his shoulders" (Isaiah 9:6).

Something Is Exaggerated for Emphasis

    a. "My eyes shed streams of water" (Psalm 119:136, NASB).
    b. "As for those agitators, I wish they would go the whole way and emasculate themselves" (Galatians 5:12).

Numbers Are Used as Symbols

In a context where symbols are consistently used, certain numbers have symbolic meanings.

    a. one—unity
    b. three—divine (Father, Son, Holy Spirit)
    c. four—earthly (four corners, four walls)
    d. ten—complete, full (derived from fingers)

e. seven—perfect, complete (derived from adding 3 and 4, divine and earthly)
f. twelve—organized religion (from 12 patriarchs and 12 apostles)
g. a thousand—period of time stretching over all generations
h. three and a half—incomplete, a short time (half of seven)
i. six—failure, sin (one short of seven)
j. 666—sin personified

It isn't always easy to tell whether a number is to be taken literally or figuratively; but if the context contains much symbolic language, chances are the number is symbolic as well.

Parables

Jesus used many parables in his teaching. Through those earthly stories he communicated eternal truths. The parable was a simple window through which Jesus enabled people to see the truth.

When seeking to understand and apply the parables, we must be careful not to get so involved in every crack and crevice of the frame that we miss seeing through the pane to the truth. Usually a parable was told for one application, which was made very clear. Do not try to make something out of every minute detail in the parable unless Jesus explained what various details meant.

Generally, you should let the context of the parable tell you the point that is being made. Often the main point was highlighted at the end of the parable. When several parables were told in a row without any intervening events, Jesus was developing a pattern of thought.

What was the meaning of Jesus' parable of the good Samaritan? (Luke 10:25-37). We must read the context carefully and notice how Jesus ended the parable. Jesus was answering the question of a lawyer: "Who is my neighbor?" Through the parable, he taught that a neighbor shows mercy on one who is in need and that the lawyer should live in the same way. This was made clear in the conversation at the end of the parable.

Luke 15 records three parables Jesus told. We must notice the context (15:1, 2) and then determine the thought pattern that is expressed. What do the first two parables have in common that the last one does not? Notice how Jesus ended the three parables (verse 32). What one truth was he communicating?

Here is a list of parables that will be helpful for you to study. Remember to note the context, search for the pattern of thought, and notice how the parable ends (often the key to the application).

The Children—Matthew 11:16-19

The Sower—Matthew 13:3-9 (see verses 18-23); Mark 4:3-8 (see verses 14-20); Luke 8:5-8 (see verses 9-15)

The Wheat and the Tares—Matthew 13:24-30 (see verses 36-43)

The Mustard Seed—Matthew 13:31, 32; Mark 4:30-32; Luke 13:18, 19

The Leaven—Matthew 13:33; Luke 13:20, 21

The Hidden Treasure—Matthew 13:44

The Pearl—Matthew 13:45, 46

The Net—Matthew 13:47-50

The Unforgiving Servant—Matthew 18:23-35

The Two Sons—Matthew 21:28-32

The Wicked Tenant Farmers—Matthew 21:33-44; Mark 12:1-12; Luke 20:9-19

The Marriage Feast—Matthew 22:1-14

The Fig Tree—Matthew 24:32, 33; Mark 13:28, 29; Luke 21:29-31

The Unfaithful Servant—Matthew 24:45-51; Luke 12:41-48

The Ten Virgins—Matthew 25:1-13

The Talents—Matthew 25:14-30

The Growing Seed—Mark 4:26-29

The Doorkeeper—Mark 13:33-37

The Rich Fool—Luke 12:13-21

The Lost Sheep—Luke 15:1-7
The Lost Coin—Luke 15:8-10
The Lost Son—Luke 15:11-32
The Rich Man and Lazarus—Luke 16:19-31
The Widow and the Judge—Luke 18:1-8
The Pharisee and the Tax Collector—Luke 18:9-14
The Sheepfold—John 10:1-6
The Good Shepherd—John 10:7-18

Conclusion

Jesus was very adept at illustrating truths. He wanted his hearers to understand. He left Heaven, put on flesh, became a servant of mankind, and lived among men as a man to communicate God's truth. He not only spoke it, he demonstrated it.

He did not go to all that trouble to leave us with an incomprehensible mess of words. He did not come to say, "You will never be able to understand God's Word." No, he came to say, "You can understand it, and it will be a blessing to you." God has spoken to everyone, no matter what his status or education. "He who has ears to hear, let him hear."

Questions for Discussion

1. It is hoped that by this time in your study of this book, your Bible reading has improved. Are you spending more time in Bible reading and study? How much time do you spend meditating on God's Word? What is the difference between reading the Bible and meditating on it?
2. Some people say you must take all the Bible literally or you rob it of its authority. Do you agree or disagree? Why?

3. The author lists several figurative phrases, or idioms, commonly used in our speech today. Why do you think we understand them so easily but have trouble understanding the idioms of the Bible?

4. Some interpreters like to take a historical event from the Bible and make it into an allegory for Christian living. Do you think this is a valid way to interpret the Bible? Why or why not? What does the author's principle on page 83 ("Interpret God's Word literally unless you have a clear reason to take it symbolically") do for this principle?

5. What is the difference between using a historical event as an illustration and using it as an allegory? Is there any more validity to one than the other? Why or why not?

6. The author points out that a parable was "usually . . . told for one application." This point is often cited as the difference between a parable and an allegory, in which every point has relevance to the application. What potential dangers can you think of in allegorizing a parable, applying every minute detail to contemporary life?

7. Are there some parables that are allegorical (several points of application instead of just one)? If so, which ones can you think of?

Step Eight

Putting It Into Practice

Why should we be concerned about applying to our daily lives what God tells us in his Word? Won't people know we are Jesus' disciples if we just love one another? (John 13:34, 35). Didn't Jesus and Paul both say that all the law and the prophets are fulfilled if we love God and our neighbor (Matthew 22:37-40; Romans 13:8-10)? Then why study? Can't we just love?

If we really are going to love one another, we must know what true love is. There have been times when I thought I was being loving, but I wasn't. Real love is unselfish service that meets the needs of another person.

In order to know about that kind of love, we need to read what God's Word says about it. God created us; he knows our needs and how best to meet them. And he has shared with us this information.

Love takes a back seat when we do not seek to understand God's Word, which reveals his will. Throughout human history, when people were without understanding they became unlovely and unmerciful. Their conduct was governed by greed, malice, and envy. It included murder, slander, and other evil deeds because their minds became depraved (Romans 1:28-32).

Paul wrote that Christians are not to continue to be children in their thinking. Our understanding is to mature. When we mature in this way, we become "infants" in doing evil (1 Corinthians 14:20), which means we are not experts at doing evil.

We simply cannot love properly without knowing Jesus, who was love in flesh. "Whoever does not love does not know God" (1 John 4:8). And we cannot love him unless we obey what he taught: "If anyone loves me, he will obey my teaching" (John 14:23).

After Jesus gave the apostles an example to remember and treasure, he said to them, "Now that you know these things, you will be blessed if you do them" (John 13:17). We are to *know* in order to *do*. Bible study is not for the purpose of filling us up with information. Being no more than a walking and talking encyclopedia of Bible facts will not make us able to meet the needs of today. What is needed is for a multitude of God's people to put into daily practice the principles communicated in the Bible!

Learning is for living. We understand so we can utilize. As soon as we discover the meaning of a Bible verse or passage, we need to ask, "How can I wrap my own skin around the truth and let it walk around in the kitchen, the living room, the shop, the park, the office, the school?"

One of the main faults of most commentaries is that they do not bridge the gap between the first-century activity and the twentieth-century application. Effective Bible study must always deal with these two questions: (1) What did this mean to the first readers? and (2) How does this apply to today's readers? There is little value in asking the first question if we fail to ask the second; but at the same time, we cannot adequately answer the second until we answer the first.

Failing to make an application to the "now" situation is probably the major pitfall in our Christian lives. Isn't it easy to listen to a good sermon or lesson without transferring the biblical principle into our own personal activities? Isn't it easy to sit comfortably and say to ourselves with assurance, "I know what that means"? But it is not so easy to get off the pew or chair and look for opportunities to live out the truth.

In fact, many of us really are not interested in implementing the meaning of Scripture, especially when we realize what utilization of a principle may demand of us. In this final "step," I want us to deal with the nitty-gritty of putting our Bible knowledge into practice. In the following paragraphs, I will discuss various sections of Scripture. Notice how tough the applications are.

Going to Court

First Corinthians 6:1-7 develops the principle of not taking a Christian brother to court to sue him. It would be better to be defrauded than to do that. To sue a brother fosters disunity in the family of God. Do you think God has changed his mind about this matter in the twentieth century?

What should you do if a brother in Christ hits your car, and he does not have insurance? What if a brother in Christ will not uphold a guarantee on a piece of equipment he has sold you? Isn't it time for the church to handle disputes between members?

Care for Aged Parents

First Timothy 5:1-16 says that grown children are to provide financial care for their aged and widowed mothers. Paul said that anyone who does not do so has denied the faith and is worse than an unbeliever (5:8). As I was growing up, I never was taught that taking care of a widowed mother would be my responsibility. If this principle is to be lived out, then we had better start teaching it in our churches now!

Do you get off the hook by letting the government do it? How impersonal! My mother never carried the government in her body for nine months; she carried me. She never got up in the middle of the night for the government, but she got up for me. We must live this principle out specifically. If you think you are giving too much to the church to help your aged parents, read what Jesus said in Matthew 15:3-14.

Unity in the Church

Ephesians 4:2 entreats us to forbear one another in love. To forbear is to "put up with" one another. Is there someone in the church you find it difficult to put up with? What can you do to put up with that one? Remember, we are on different spiritual levels. Some in the church are still babes; they need direction from someone more mature.

Verses 11 through 16 in Ephesians 4 suggest that all of us have different gifts or abilities. Each of us is a member of the body of Christ. Are you a contributing member? Are you sharing your abilities with others? If you aren't, the growth of Christ's body is being stunted.

List the abilities you know you have (baking pies, fixing cars, painting, making others feel good, or something else). Then list how you can help others with your abilities. And then decide when this next week you will do it!

We can get angry. Isn't that great news? But we are commanded to get rid of our anger before the sun sets that day (Ephesians 4:26). Uh, oh! That's bad news. We might as well not get mad at all; the sun goes down so soon!

Wouldn't it be great if every time we saw the sunset, we immediately took stock to determine whether there was disharmony between ourselves and someone else and then made an attempt to make things right? How can we get over our anger? Often it is best to talk it over with the person we are angry with (Matthew 5:22-25). We should look for the wrong we did and admit it (James 5:16). If we were clearly wronged, we should not try to get even (1 Peter 2:21-23). Be willing to be insulted. Jesus was mistreated wrongly and did not fight back.

Our tongue is to be used for building up another person, not for tearing him down (Ephesians 4:29). How is your tongue-life? What do you say about others? Do you find fault with them or praise them? Do you pass on rumors? Few things can poison our minds and characters more surely than wrong talk. Few things can destroy the love and unity of a church as quickly as maliciously wagging tongues.

The Bible—Our Great Treasure

Bible study is mind-expanding and life-changing. It gives us new insights and illuminates new directions for our living.

The greatest way I demonstrate that I love my father is to imitate him. I cannot imitate him unless I know him. And the only way to know him is by spending a lot of time with him, listening to him and watching him as he lives.

We all are pressing on toward the goal of being like our Father in Heaven. We are endeavoring to grow up to be like Christ, who showed us God in flesh. We want to imitate him.

The Bible is not just paper and ink. It is a living Word that reveals to us what God thinks and does. It allows the mind of God to become our mind. It is the tool through which the Holy Spirit renews our minds and transforms us into his image.

But the Bible alone is not enough. We need each other also. The Holy Spirit lives in each Christian, and we all are connected to the head of the body—Christ. But we are held together by that which every member supplies (Ephesians 4:16, especially as translated in the NASB).

So don't get off in a corner of the world and just read the Bible. If the Bible is effective in your life, you will become involved in the lives of people. You will become a better wife, husband, mother, father, friend, neighbor, employer, employee, child, teacher, student.

The Bible is not to make us scholars, but servants. "For who is greater, the one who is at the table, or the one who serves? Is it not the one who is at the table? But I am among you as one who serves" (Luke 22:27). When we can say, "We are among you as ones who serve," then and only then have we allowed the Bible to get out of its first-century culture and into the twentieth-century fabric of our lives.

Attitudes Toward Study

If you want to be loving, you must understand God's Word and apply it. But don't let that scare you. You don't even have to be an elementary school graduate to understand God's Word.

Jesus once said, "I praise you, Father, Lord of heaven and earth, because you have hidden these things from the wise and learned, and revealed them to little children" (Matthew 11:25, 26). *Little children* here refers to people who were humble and ready to learn. The *wise* and *learned* were those who already had their minds made up and could not be taught by anyone. Jesus was not contrasting PhD's with high-school dropouts, but intellectual pride with humility.

I have known some people with PhD degrees who were humble and ready to study and learn from God's Word; I have also known some high-school dropouts who were so arrogant that they thought they knew all there was to know about the Bible. The arrogant ones are the bullies of the church. They want to dominate rather than to learn. We don't see love in their actions and attitudes.

No matter who you are, you can know God's Word if you admit you have a lot to learn and if your mind is open to learn. Your attitude makes the difference.

Questions for Discussion

1. The author says we cannot really love God or one another without a good understanding of the Bible. Do you agree or disagree? Why? What points does the author make to support his claim?
2. Why do you think "failing to make the application to the 'now' situation" is so common? (The author calls it the "major pitfall in our Christian lives.") Are church leaders or the people in the pews more responsible for this failure? Why?
3. The author makes an appeal for the church to handle disputes between members so they would not have to go to court (based on 1 Corinthians 6:1-7). If the church will not handle the dispute, is it then okay to go to court? Why or why not? What if the parties are from different churches?
4. Do you think the prohibition of going to court applies to criminal cases as well as to civil suits? In other words, should a Christian not press charges against a Christian brother or sister who has committed a criminal act against him? Should the church be prepared to handle such "disputes"? Why or why not?
5. Do you think a son or daughter should refuse government aid to help aged parents? (See 1 Timothy 5:1-16.) If the parent is eligible for such aid, isn't it just good stewardship to take the money and then add to it from one's own resources? Why or why not?
6. What do you see as the greatest threat to unity in the church? What can be done about the issue?
7. The author says "your attitude [about Bible study] makes the difference." What difference does attitude make? How do the following attitudes help or hinder Bible study?
   a. Pride
   b. Self-confidence
   c. Low self-esteem
   d. Openness

e. Fear

f. Eagerness

8. Here are some texts to read and apply specifically to yourself. Ask these questions of each text: What does it teach? What will I do to apply it? To whom? How? And when?

a. Matthew 5:27-32; 6:1, 25; 7:15

b. Romans 12:6-8, 10, 16, 17; 14:13, 19; 15:1, 2, 7

c. Galatians 3:28; 5:15; 6:1, 2

d. Philippians 2:3, 4

e. 1 Timothy 1:3, 4; 5:17-19

f. James 2:1-6, 15, 16

g. 1 Peter 2:1, 2; 5:1-4